THOU SHALL KNOT IN LOVE AND MARRIAGE

*TYING THE KNOT BY EXCHANGING FRANK AND FORMATIVE "F" WORDS

BY JOHN H. GREEN, PHD

Order this book online at www.trafford.com/08-0955
or email orders@trafford.com

Most Trafford titles are also available at major online book retailers.

Designed by: Kay M. Green

Edited by: Judy Head

Note for Librarians: A cataloguing record for this book is available from Library and Archives Canada at www.collectionscanada.ca/amicus/index-e.html

ISBN: 978-1-4251-8277-9

We at Trafford believe that it is the responsibility of us all, as both individuals and corporations, to make choices that are environmentally and socially sound. You, in turn, are supporting this responsible conduct each time you purchase a Trafford book, or make use of our publishing services. To find out how you are helping, please visit www.trafford.com/responsiblepublishing.html

Our mission is to efficiently provide the world's finest, most comprehensive book publishing service, enabling every author to experience success. To find out how to publish your book, your way, and have it available worldwide, visit us online at www.trafford.com/10510

www.trafford.com

North America & international
toll-free: 1 888 232 4444 (USA & Canada)
phone: 250 383 6864 • fax: 250 383 6804 • email: info@trafford.com

The United Kingdom & Europe
phone: +44 (0)1865 487 395 • local rate: 0845 230 9601
facsimile: +44 (0)1865 481 507 • email: info.uk@trafford.com

10 9 8 7 6 5 4 3 2

COMMENT

DEAR JOHN,

Thanks for inviting me to read a copy of your book. In addition to the enjoyment of reading it, I felt we were in conversation, and that was also enjoyable.

First of all, I think it is well written. I like the brevity, levity, and practicality of the book. All three of these things make it a good "niche" book among the many that have been published on marriage. Too many others are too long, too psychological, or too academic for the average young couple to wade through. The brief, practical, and sometimes funny things you say make it both readable and understandable. It doesn't have to be deciphered. If as many people are geared to quick messages as the pundits say, then your book has a lot of good things to say in a short and memorable form. Also, you are not saying, "If you want a happy marriage this is what you have to do." It is more like saying here are a lot of things many of us have experienced and worked out over time; hope it will help you.

I like your play on the "F" word. It's an attention grabber, but a valid way to approach those subjects. I also like the use of I Corinthians 13. Most non-religious people appreciate it, and it does add authentication for the religious.

I also like the summary and the questions at the end of each chapter. They provide a good review for a couple or a group.

My own thoughts are that men and women view sex and marriage so differently, that it would be a great benefit to young men and women if they were taught these differences from the beginning.

I have finally boiled down my pre-marital talk to say that they should learn to talk to each other, fight fair, make love, and have fun with each other. Each is an art and has to be learned. Don't get discouraged, but just keep trying. Each has to realize the other is totally different, and that neither can read each other's mind. I'm still learning after 55 years of marriage!

The Reverend Dr. Gene Zimmerman
Retired Minister, The United Methodist Church

This book is dedicated
to my wife
Kay Miller Green

ACKNOWLEDGEMENTS

I WOULD LIKE to express my appreciation to several friends in writing this book. First, I would like to thank The Reverend Dr. Gene Zimmerman and his wife Emily Ann for reading my first manuscript and reflecting their thoughts, and offering ideas to the project. Kay and I have known Gene and Emily Ann for nearly thirty years, and they have been good friends and mentors to the both of us. Gene performed our wedding ceremony on June 3, 1983.

I am very grateful to Judy Head for reading and assisting in editing my work. Judy is presently a high school teacher who has taught both English and Mathematics. She and her husband Al live in Montgomery, Alabama, and we have been friends for nearly thirty years.

I am dedicating this book to my wife Kay of nearly twenty-six years. She and I have worked hard to establish a blended family with love and appreciation for our children, Robin Bowman and Bryan Ellison. Robin has a Master's Degree and her husband Chris has a Ph.D. They have three children, Elie, Kate and Jack. Bryan and his wife Nicole both have Civil Engineering Degrees. They have a daughter named Sienna.

I am blessed to be a stepfather and a step-grandfather. They all bring joy to my life and are a pleasure to know and love. Every holiday allows us time with one or the other, but it is never long enough. However, each meeting means more and more as time moves on, and hopefully in the future, each moment will be will even more valuable with each time we gather.

Thanks always to several friends and families who have contributed unknowingly to this project through my performing their marriages, counseling with them, and giving me the honor and privilege to have been a part of their lives. The numbers over the years are too many to mention, but they have helped me enjoy the journey of life through love and marriage. Their contribution has made the knot in my marriage stronger.

ABOUT THE AUTHOR

DR. JOHN H. Green is a fulltime Professor at St. Johns River Community College in St. Augustine, Florida. He teaches Fundamentals of Public Speaking and Debate and Argumentation. Dr. Green is faculty advisor for the Speech Club and devotes time as the debate coach. He received his Ph.D. from Florida State University in 1981.

Dr. Green was recommended to *Who's Who Among America's Teachers* in 2003-04 by students when he taught at Jacksonville University in Jacksonville, Florida. He was recommended for the same award in 2004-05 by the students at the community college. In 2006 the Student Government Association at St. Johns River Community College voted him Professor of the Year.

Dr. Green has spent over forty years working in churches and schools. He also has a Master's Degree in Divinity and a Master's Degree in Christian Education from Emory University, located outside of Atlanta, Georgia. Dr. Green is author of numerous newspaper and magazine articles. He also authored the book, *Elder Cool Time,* available through local bookstores and Trafford Publishing.

Dr. Green says, "College students keep me thinking young, and keep me on my toes in the classroom. The students are not just America's future, but the present as well. Deal with these minds in the present and the world will be better and safer in the future. I struggle to engage myself with the students in a way that teaches them to think 'outside the bun.' In doing so creative minds will bring all of us a destiny of a hope that will never die. I also teach that humor is a great source for loving to learn, that humility will help keep a balance in life, and that serving humanity will bring a sense of peace and happiness."

THOU SHALL KNOT IN LOVE AND MARRIAGE

---

*TYING THE KNOT
BY EXCHANGING FRANK AND FORMATIVE "F" WORDS.

BY JOHN H. GREEN, PHD

CONTENTS

INTRODUCTION

"Love is patient; love is kind; love is not envious or boastful or arrogant or rude.
It does not insist on its own way; it is not irritable or resentful;
it does not rejoice in wrongdoing, but rejoices in the truth. It bears all things,
believes all things, hopes all things, and endures all things.
Love never ends."

I CORINTHIANS 13:4-8; 14:1 (NRSV)

ADVICE FOR LOVERS

Marriage ceremonies for kings and queens, prince and princesses, and the common people all over the world, have included marriage vows previewed by I Corinthians 13. This is the greatest definition of love. Christian love is a love that develops beyond the usual erotic action demonstrated and paraded as love. Some people believe a good sneeze is underrated and good sex is overrated. Personally, I don't accept that. No one says, "Gesundheit" after good sex. If the sex is good, you sing "Hallelujah"! Love in the popular scripture of Corinthians is more than sex and romance. "Puppy Love" is part of nature, but it is very short of true love. Love is a fact of life that includes procreation and recreation. Realizing the need and separation of each is a good sign of maturity in marriage, or any loving and caring relationship. Practicing the words of I Corinthians 13 with the deeds of love is good advice for all lovers married or not.

A friend told me the story of two elderly men who were discussing how long they had been married. One of them commented he had been married for fifty years. After his comment, he stated, "You know I can remember where I was married, and I can remember when I was married, but for the life of me, I cannot remember why I was married."

Although a smile may cross our faces, NEVER forget why you married! And LOVE better be the answer. There is an old saying that marriages are made in heaven, but must be worked out on earth. Love, the kind mentioned in I Corinthians 13, can help work through the worst of relationships.

The purpose of the booklet is to incorporate some frank and formative "F" words into the viewpoint of love found in I Corinthians 13. This is a possible study guide with discussion questions, and a possible counseling supplement for those who may be thinking of marriage and are in a relationship, as well as those who are married and trying to work it out. Exchanging these words may have a positive effect on relationships.

FLEXIBILITY

Marriage is a test of patience. Patience is a virtue, according to an old saying, and lack of patience is a venom attack, worse than a rattlesnake bite. Therefore, the value of flexibility is priceless. Unless one can learn the value of flexibility, patience may never be a virtue in your interpersonal relationships. Understanding and accepting another person's limitation leads towards patience. Since each person is a special creation of the Almighty, love is patient. Love is flexible.

An elderly clergyman preached a wonderful sermon on marriage. After the worship service a church member asked how long he had taken to prepare such a sermon. The minister replied, "All my life." Learning patience in marriage may take all your life. Better start now!

FAIRNESS

There is another widespread thought that the one who has the TV remote is in control of the household. Hold that thought and you will eventually be without the house, TV, and remote. A spouse who continually seeks control within the relationship stands to lose the concept of love. Love is kind. Love must play fair.

The story is told that the wife of Mark Twain was a very controlling person. She insisted he wear the proper clothes when visiting the neighbors. Mark Twain would have preferred to dress more comfortably. One day when he visited a neighbor without a collar and tie, she scolded him. Mark Twain responded by wrapping the collar and tie and sending them to the neighbor with a note, "I visited you without my collar and tie. The articles are enclosed. Will you kindly gaze at them for thirty minutes and return them to me?"

FOOLING AROUND

Sexual intimacy is more than just relieving tensions. It is a portion of romance that involves the deepest emotions. Men and women need and respond differently in regards to sexuality. Human sexuality is for recreation and procreation. When couples understand each other's sexual needs then lovemaking is more satisfactory for both partners. Then love is not resentful or irritable. Mutual understanding can lead to the truth found in the thinking that good sex is good and bad sex is good.

FIGHTING

Fighting is allowed, to the amazement of some. Fighting does not include verbal or physical abuse. The lesson of fighting is to know the boundaries that should exist with each other. Keeping everything inside can eventually lead to a war of the roses. Know what buttons NOT to push. Communication is more than a casual word to be taken lightly. If love is to endure, then the ability to care and to share will lead to the fruits of the endurance.

Avoid the accusation of being the partner some seaman refer to in life as, "The oyster is not the only one who has a crab for a mate."

FIDELITY

Fooling around belongs only to committed partners. Marriage is a total commitment to the love of another. Fidelity is the foundation of total trust. Trust is love and love bears all things. The unfaithful break the cords of trust and the result can be disastrous. Once this happens, should the truth be told? A marriage does not rejoice in wrongdoing, but rejoices in that which is right. Should one tell the truth about infidelity to solve one's own feelings of guilt? "Infidelity...nullifies every blessing." Pestalozzi

FINANCE

The love of money is said to be the root of evil. Not money, but the LOVE of money is the root of evil. Money problems create marital problems. Period! A wealth of money can bring boastful, and sometimes, arrogant attitudes. A fantasy of money, on the other hand, when money is not available as wished, can cause stretch marks on the credit cards. The lack of financial communication between partners can result in a futile attempt for happiness in a long lasting relationship.

FRIENDSHIP

There is a Japanese proverb, "Love without friendship is like a shadow without the sun." Friendship can contribute to a never-ending love because the pangs of emotions are torpedoed with the closeness of friendship. Many lovers know the value of friendship as first and foremost in a relationship. However, if friendship is not at the beginning of love, friendship can become a growth process in the partnership.

FUN

Life will always have enough serious times. That seriousness includes interpersonal relationships. Therefore, partners need some fun time. It is very easy to get in a rut. As the old V8 juice commercial shouts, "Get out of the rut." You can have tomato juice just so often!

Every time I hear a recording of Frank Sinatra, I know why I am not a singer. But the Karaoke machine can be a lot of fun. I know a couple that thoroughly enjoy each other and have a lot of fun with Karaoke. I also know that Frank Sinatra's musical legend will not be challenged, but oh they have so much fun.

FAITH

There is more to a marriage than a mattress. The physical is good, but the spiritual is longer lasting. I believe that faith is to the spiritual realm like sex is to the physical realm. As taught by scripture, love is the greatest of all. Perhaps the strongest of these is faith. It takes more than a firm mattress to ensure a good night's sleep.

FUTURE

What is your future in life with a partner? That is, do you vision where you want to be in five, ten years, or more? Poor eyesight limits your vision. Poor vision limits your life.

Your marriage success may depend on your vision for the future. A vision can lead a couple to a never-ending love.

CONCLUSION

The "F" words are not intended to solve all problems of interpersonal relationships, and especially marriages. This booklet is intended to raise levels of influence and awareness in relationships. All human relationships are difficult. Even the best intentions in a marriage sometimes trigger negative responses. However, the desires to seek a positive relationship in all partnerships will make a major difference in improving the relations.

Note the discussion questions at the end of each chapter. These questions can encourage communication between couples in a way that might just spark some renewed excitement in the marriage. The more one personalizes the matters in each chapter, the greater the possible benefits. Use this booklet to set out on a journey to discover yourself and the possible improvement of relating to a significant other. As you travel include the significant other while making love your aim and THOU SHALL KNOT!

LOVE IS PATIENT

1

FLEXIBILITY

"I'm extraordinarily patient, provided I get my own way in the end."
MARGARET THATCHER

ALLOWING SPACE

There are moments when a partner cries, "I am suffocating." The partner may feel trapped or locked in without a chance to move around the world. A lack of freedom to be one's self can be emotionally overcoming. The need for personal freedom is a product of securing a personal identity. Togetherness is a wonderful feeling, but so is the flexibility to have space in a relationship. Togetherness and space are emotional twins.

Togetherness and space don't appear to belong in the same boat, but emotionally they do. A successful marriage requires both. Flexibility is a key to the ignition. Flexibility does not come without a price. Patience is the price. Maturity requires space allowing growth as an individual and growth within the relationship. Flexibility allows the space to happen. Space in time does not always come at a convenient time for both.

A boy's night out is healthy. A girl's night out is also healthy in a mature relationship. Some husbands and wives view this as a threat. Certainly a mature relationship requests limitations and boundaries to such freedoms. Knowing when and where a partner is going represents the limitations and boundaries, and is a simple matter of respect. This builds trust.

The police have on file the story of a husband who drove to the police station one evening and asked to speak to the guy who was arrested for breaking into his house. "What for?" inquired a police officer.

The husband responded, "I would like to know how he got into the house without waking my wife."

When married people are strong individuals, they will begin the normal process of allowing space soon after the marriage begins. Mates will trust one another and will not mind brief periods of absence. Such freedom creates a higher level of marital maturity.

In giving space, a partner should not leave for outer space. Space in time is a cop out time for some. Partners need to be perfectly clear on the expectations of togetherness and space. George Eliot wrote, "It's easy finding reasons why other folks should be patient." When agreed on expectations are neglected in the equation to space in time, patience is tested to the boiling point and trust is threatened. Obviously, if one person is refusing to be cooperative in the expectations, the "other" one should be patient!

Lawyer: "You say you want to get a divorce on the grounds that your husband is careless about his appearance?"
Client: "Yes, he has not appeared for almost five years."

ALLOWING CHANGE

The roles of men and women are changing. Sometimes our socialization has not prepared us to function in the new roles of husbands and wives. A shift in responsibilities is difficult for some. Jobs around the house should be shared. This should to be a no brain decision if both partners work outside the home.

Anyone who visits malls and shopping centers today, and enters a restroom while shopping, will often find a "change the baby's diaper room" in the men's room. The roles continue to change and they should. It's been said that a baby is the only one who likes change. Human nature usually dictates a refusal or hesitancy to change. A wife hung an attention getting slogan in the house, "Prayer changes things." The husband immediately took it down.

Surprised, the wife asked, "Don't you believe in prayer?"

"Yes," he responded, "but I don't believe in change."

Spouses should allow the rearrangement of rights and responsibilities in order to experience space, growth, and a certain amount of independence. Allowing change allows time for self-discovery. Opposing change will build barriers within the relationship and block communication. The derailing of communication leads to a lack of mutual understanding. In the words of Woodrow Wilson, "Patience comes to those who wait." Waiting may include serious observation of a situation before deciding one cannot live with certain changes that evolve naturally in partnerships. Therefore, while waiting, flexibility becomes the best friend of patience.

A fellow named David said he decided on marriage because he was tired of washing his own clothes, eating out all the time, and doing nothing but watching the television. Another fellow named Jim said he decided on divorce for the same reasons! David is blind to the real expectations of marriage and certainly has no sight on marrying for the right reasons. Jim is also blind to sharing responsibilities and obviously knows nothing of love. Both guys are in for a major change whether in marriage or divorce.

If love for one another is true, then respect of needs and desires of both parties is needed. Changes are not always progressive, but change is going to happen and can be healthy in a marriage. Ambrose Bierce, defined patience, as, "A minor form of despair disguised as a virtue." Patience may be too often couched in despair, but "minor" is the key word, and virtue will win out if love is the aim in the relationship.

ALLOWING INDIVIDUALITY

People in a relationship walk a tight line trying to balance unity and individuality. Individuality is extremely important to each partner, but cannot be allowed to extinguish the unity of the marriage. In each individual there is more than one person. Discovering and allowing these different persons to exist in a marriage is no less than a challenge of patience. Sometimes the wife may need to be a "little girl" and the husband a "little boy". This is not okay if the "little girl" or "little boy" comes often and stays long. Actually, this is unhealthy.

Within most of us exists a happy person and, at other times, a person of anxiety. Some of us are combating within us an extravert and an introvert, knowing that one is often more powerful than the other on certain days and in certain situations. Some people battle the demons of being too impulsive or too compulsive. When the immovable objects meet the irresistible forces within, can a partner accept the individuals within the individual? Usually patience and love are tested, but can be arrested, if the partners are willing to be flexible.

The words of the prophet Kahilil Gibran place a positive perspective on individuality and unity:

Then Almitra spoke again and said, "And what of marriage, Master?"
And he answered:

"You were born together, and together you shall be forevermore.
You shall be together when the white wings of death scatter your days.
Aye, you shall be together even in the silent memory of God.
But let there be spaces in your togetherness.
And let the winds of the heavens dance between you.
Love one another but make not a bond of love:
Let it rather be a moving sea between the shores of your souls.
Fill each other's cup but drink not from one cup.
Give one another of your bread but eat not from the same loaf.
Sing and dance together and be joyous, but let each one of you be alone,
Even as the things of a lute are alone though they quiver with the same music.
Give your hearts, but not into each other's keeping.
For only the hand of God can contain your hearts.
And stand together, yet not too near together:
For the pillars of the temple stand apart,
And the oak tree and the cypress grow not in each other's shadow."

Everyone has frailties and failures. No one is perfect and imperfections reveal vulnerabilities. The expansion of our individuality within a relationship helps to deal with vulnerability. Pretending to be something a person is not is a trap, but being able to take off the masks gives a stronger self-image in the long run, most of the time. Maintaining the unity in the relationship at the same time creates a stronger interpersonal relationship. Individuality does not have to be viewed as selfishness when partners accept the premise of unity and individuality. Flexibility provides for space and love to grow together. Seeking space and love helps to maintain a happy marriage.

SUMMARY

Flexibility in a marriage allows partners to have their space. Allowing space takes patience, but it leads to a more mature relationship. Respect and trust are built in the partnership when the space is allowed. Limitations and boundaries are recommended for space in time. Spouses need clear communication on togetherness and unity.

Marital roles where males and females are involved with responsibilities need to know times are a changing. Peace and happiness comes to those who accept the possibilities of change, and embrace the changes with grace and understanding.

There is a tight line to walk and to balance unity and individuality in a relationship. Whether an individual wants to believe it or not, more than one individual exists in each person. Accepting the different individuals by each partner creates a home acceptable to flexibility. Unity and individuality can live and stand together in a marriage of sincere dedication.

> *"And stand together, yet not too near together.*
> *For the pillars of the temple stand apart,*
> *And the oak tree and the cypress grow not in each other's shadow."*
>
> KHILIL GIBRAN

DISCUSSION QUESTIONS

FLEXIBILITY

Allowing Space

1. Are you suffocating in your relationship?
2. How can togetherness and space be emotional twins?
3. Do you believe in a boy's and a girl's night out?
4. Do you have times apart devoted to learning, searching, and fulfilling needs?
5. Do you set boundaries and limits to your space in time?

Allowing Change

1. How do you feel about the different roles of men and women today?
2. Do you have the flexibility in your relationship to discover your identity?
3. How do you feel about the comments of David or Jim?
4. Why did you get married or want to get married?
5. What are your expectations in a marriage?

Allowing Individuality

1. How do you cope with unity and individuality?
2. Are you aware that more than one individual exists within you?
3. Can you describe the different persons within you?
4. Can you accept the different persons in your partner?
5. What is your viewpoint of the prophet Gibran?

LOVE IS KIND

2

FAIRNESS

"So many gods, so many creeds,
So many paths that wind and wind,
While just the art of being kind
Is all the sad world needs."

ELLA W. WILCOX

LETTING GO OF CONTROL

Two husbands were talking about the subject of hypnotism and one asked, "What does it mean to be hypnotized?"

The husband who appeared to know everything, replied, "To hypnotize is to get a person in your control, and then make that person do whatever you want."

Astonished, the other husband said, "That's not hypnotism, that's marriage."

Getting someone to follow one's way all the time is a negative power force in a relationship. Marital duels occur over, "Who's in control?" The control factor diminishes the power of love. Sometimes one partner has to let go of their ego. Egos cancel fairness. The TV remote can change the marriage instead of the channel. They can be minor for the moment, but these little things accumulate, and over time the little becomes big.

No one should view a partnership from the "I am in charge" status. Marriage is not about control, but it is about fairness. Marriage is about kindness. Marriage is about love. Living together without one partner having the "upper hand" is a sign of maturity.

Letting go of control begins with listening. To listen involves reaching a mutual understanding. Communication is really a process including continuous feedback. Lack of feedback breaks down the process of communication and blocks the path to mutual understanding. Listening includes watching the body language of your partner, the tone of voice, and then responding appropriately. Nonverbal communication affects verbal communication. Speech experts believe facial expressions are the most telling of nonverbal feedback. Listening is more than just listening to words.

A wife had been talking for about ten minutes when she realized her husband was not listening or looking at her. He was completely absorbed in the newspaper. She questioned, "Why don't you answer me?"

"I did," he shot back. "I shook my head no," he said abruptly.

"Well pardon me, but I didn't hear your brain rattling," she said.

Most are guilty when it comes to a failure in listening to our partners. The lack of a hearing aid is not always the problem. However, the lack of fairness, a neglect of kindness, is a problem. When a person fails to listen to the significant other, he or she is being rude. Love is not arrogant or rude. To walk away while one is trying to communicate lowers the level of fairness. It is not fair to allow only one-sided communication. A non-caring attitude is formulated when kindness is forfeited. Love will be doubted when time is not taken to demonstrate fairness.

Whenever there is a need to communicate there is the responsibility of both partners to stop whatever they are doing to show kindness. Most people have certain needs and concerns that might come at an inconvenient time, but to neglect that need or concern devastates the relationship of caring. If love is kindness then care must be demonstrated. The demonstration of care releases the need to control.

Singer and songwriter, Paul Simon, had a hit song titled, *Fifty Ways to Leave Your Lover.* Some of these lyrics suggest our attention. For example, "hop on the bus, Gus, don't need to discuss much." "Don't need to discuss much" grabs my attention. Happy marriages take time to discuss much, especially needs and concerns.

LIVING KINDNESS

My wife and I have developed "little" loves and "big" loves over the years. The "little" loves begin each morning with coffee! She generally serves the first cup, and then I serve the second cup and so on. There have been times when one of us has been sick and one takes care of the other. One realizes after years of marriage that marriage is not a 50/50 proposition, but sometimes 90/100 or 100/0. That's fairness.

We have also experienced "big" loves as well. In 1994 I had surgery and Kay cared for me for several days. A year later Kay had major surgery and I cared for her for several weeks. When couples practice the "little" loves, then the "big" loves are easier.

Kay's father cared for her mother for over ten years after a serious stroke. She could not talk or walk without a lot of therapy and attention. I have never witnessed anyone more devoted to a loved one. The night Kay's mother died I was touched by her father's words: "I tucked her in and gave her some goodnight sugar before I left the hospital. She died during the night." Kay's father died of a heart attack not long after at the age of 84. No one has said so, but I believe a part of his death was related to a broken heart.

I will forever remember my father caring for my mom eighteen months after she was diagnosed with liver and colon cancer. She died at the tender age of 68. I had never seen dad cry for so long and so often. His demonstration of a "big" love will be impressed on my mind for an eternity.

Our parents lived kindness and in turn taught us through their example of living kindness. Their love was not always perfect, but when the going got tough, their love could suffice and reign in their marital commitment. Their fairness defined kindness.

Kindness creates fairness. A relationship without a mission of fairness leaves the relationship void of love. Criticism and sarcasm ruin many a marriage and destroys the deeds of kindness. Acts of kindness must carry with them words of kindness. Living kindness also includes words that do not put down the partner, resulting in lower self-esteem and self-confidence. Curt and sometimes cute feedback, like, "I was just joking," doesn't cut it if this is a habitual comeback. Watching what is said, as well as what is done, is imperative.

Wife: "How do you like the potato salad, dear?"

Husband: "Delicious! Did you buy it yourself?"

Constructive suggestions, not criticisms, are different. Everyone should be willing to learn. Constructive suggestions teach, in a healthy way, to help each partner grow in the relationship. Suggestions that are constructive should not come across as bossing, nagging, or demanding. That would be criticism at its worst. Who would want to be known as a Master Sergeant in a relationship?

Sarcastic criticism on a continued basis will lead to the death of a marriage. At best, these criticisms can create a wound that, even if it heals, will leave a large and long memory scar. Such criticism prevents a partner to rise up from a stream of negative behavior.

Living kindness requires a great deal of "little" loves and "big" loves. Criticism, without healthy motivations, and sarcasm, regardless of the motivation, runs the risk of an unhappy marriage.

LEAVING OUT OBEY

A prospective bride came to see me about setting a date to wed. During our conversation she asked if I would use vows including the word "obey" in the marriage ceremony. Her fiancé had insisted the word "obey" be included in the vows made to him, but not his vows to her. My answer was "No!" She began to cry and stated the fiancé would not marry her if she did not wish to say she would obey him. My thought was, "Better you learn the true love of this monster now rather than later."

When love, comfort, and honor are pledged to one another, there is no place for one partner to hold power over another. This is simply not fair. A loving kindness will not allow that one must obey the other. The only place for obedience is in one's relationship to the Creator. Love and honor in a marriage create a place of fairness in the partnership.

A renewal of vows is a good thing to do over the years. Couples need reminders of their commitment in the relationship. Hearing aloud the exchange of vows in the presence of friends and family is emotionally moving. The reminder seeks to continue the bonds of love established some time ago. Remember these traditional words?

> *"To have and to hold, from this day forward, for better or worse, for richer or poorer, in sickness and in health, to love and to cherish, till death us do part, according to God's holy command, I pledge you my faith."*

These words remind us of a time and place when partners stood face to face committed to each other. A romantic mood can be enhanced at any time by saying these words to your spouse. Marriage is a legal process that is confirmed by governmental laws, but the spirit and the love committed to each other is most important. God's ordination through the church does not disallow partners stating their vows at any time they choose. The words will find a special place in the heart of lovers and will continue to define kindness. The legal process becomes sacred with acts of kindness.

Obedience does not fit into the vows of commitment. Obedience sets up a barrier that dismantles kindness. The moment kindness is dismantled is the moment that despair in the relationship comes aboard. Obedience, on the other hand, is slave mentality and does not belong on the love boat. Marriage is not a slave relationship.

An American tourist was shocked to see a man riding a burro while the man's wife was walking behind him.

"Why doesn't your wife get to ride the burro?" the tourist demanded.

The man replied, "She doesn't own a burro."

If you think this is exaggerated, then think again. After over thirty-five years of counseling couples I have witnessed some similar situations. For example, when a new car is purchased, who drives the new car the most? Numerous examples of insensitivity in marriage, relating to rights of fairness, communicate dominance of one person over another, or the feeling of playing "second fiddle." Dominance is not love because love is kindness.

SUMMARY

"The force be with you" should be left to Luke Skywalker. Power force does not belong in a marriage. Learning to live together is not an arena for getting the "upper hand." Letting go of pride and the ego is a sure sign of maturity. Letting go of control includes developing better listening skills. Listening skills include the verbal and the nonverbal.

Letting go of control also includes giving time to the needs and concerns of the partner in need. "Don't need to discuss much." Is this a fair assumption? Not! Caring for the other demonstrates fairness.

Constructive suggestions do not allow bossing, nagging, or demanding. Sarcasm can be the death of communication in a relationship. Tone of voice is a part of the need to be caring. Living kindness requires a great many "little" loves and "big" loves.

The word "obey" does not belong in the marriage vows. Using tactics of obedience in a partnership creates a slave relationship. The renewal of marriage vows is an excellent way to spark romance, and remind couples of the time and place that they committed to each other face to face. Love is kind. Love is fair.

DISCUSSION QUESTIONS

FAIRNESS

Letting Go Of Control

1. Who dominates the TV remote in your household?
2. Do you practice listening in your marriage? Define listening.
3. Do you take time to pay attention in the real time of need?
4. What is your body language and tone of voice when communicating?
5. What is your idea of compromise?

Living Kindness

1. Name at least two "little" loves in your relationship?
2. Do you remember "big" loves in your marriage? Name a couple.
3. Discuss your parents or guardians. Were they positive role models?
4. How do you feel about the power of unkind words and sarcasm?
5. Can you think of some random deeds of kindness appropriate for marriage?

Leaving Out Obey

1. Do you really expect your spouse to obey you?
2. What does love and honor mean to you?
3. Discuss your understanding of obedience to God?
4. Have you ever renewed your marriage vows?
5. Discuss with your partner the idea of renewing marriage vows.

LOVE IS NOT ENVIOUS OR BOASTFUL OR ARROGANT OR RUDE

3

FOOLING AROUND

"Sex without love is as hollow and ridiculous as love without sex."
HUNTER S. THOMPSON, AMERICAN WRITER

"You mustn't force sex to do the work of love or love to do the work of sex."
MARY MCCARTHY, AMERICAN NOVELIST

LOVING

Human sexuality should not be separated from love. At the same time, love is more than human sexuality. Usually, when partners do not focus on love in a whole and spiritual manner, then human sexuality faces a lack of interest. It is difficult for sex to stand alone in a marriage without love.

The obscene "F" word is not used here in the context of enjoying human sexuality, but human intimacy and sexuality are enjoyment found in "fooling around." Fooling around defines the recreation involved in making love as well as the spirit intended for procreation. It's the recreation that has been depressed by religious rules of foolishness that take the fun out of human sexuality. Fooling around may not even be sexual intercourse, but simply the enjoyment created by loving the presence of a person. Loving the presence of a partner is the evolvement of a positive and mature relationship. Sexual fun is not always sexual intercourse.

In the words of Henry Ward Beecher, "Love is not a possession, but a growth." Therefore, if partners work to equate love with sex, and without force, there are rewards of a long and successful relationship. If the sexual fires wane soon after the commitment of love is made to one another, then growth has been neglected.

Anonymous once wrote, "Love is the fire of life; it either consumes or purifies." Equating love with sex offers the thought that the fire in sex also can consume or purify. Purification would be the better when purification means sex is more than a physical contact and more like a loving encounter.

"Love looks through a telescope; envy through a microscope," says Josh Billings, American writer. In using Mr. Billings quote in the context of more open-minded thinking, loving should not have to deal with envy. Envy, within a loving relationship, seeks to attack our securities and raise the level of our insecurities so high that the light of love can be extinguished. The scriptural text in I Corinthians 13 has little to do with what love is in relation to human sexuality, but if one looks at what love is NOT, then the view through the telescope is applicable. "Love is not envy," the scripture teaches us, and applies to any and every part of love's relationship to human sexuality.

"Love is never without jealousy," says James Kelly in *Complete Collections of Scottish Proverbs.* Jealousy and envy, for many, are cut from the same mold. Assuming the close relationship between the two, what is it that allows these two devils to enter a loving relationship? And how do these devils affect love and human sexuality? The answer to both questions lies in the satisfaction of the sexual encounters with lovers. Whose pleasure is this sexual act anyway?

"There is more pleasure in loving, than in being loved," wrote Thomas Fuller. This quote is a telescope remark. Satisfaction is achieved when both partners believe there is more pleasure in loving than in being loved. Regardless of the attempts to have a satisfactory sex life, envy and jealousy will raise their snake like heads and discharge venom into the best of loving partners. Temptation moving toward infidelity is the breeding ground for jealousy and envy. The LACK of sexual satisfaction, and little communication between partners involving their sexual feelings, opens the door to envy and jealousy as they are coupled by temptation.

MAKING LOVE

"There are a number of mechanical devices which increase sexual arousal... Chief among these is the Mercedes-Benz..." P.J. O'Rourke, American writer

"More divorces start in the bedroom than in any other room in the house." Ann Landers, American writer

"You don't need a Harvard MBA to know that the bedroom and the boardroom are just two sides of the same ball game." Stephen Fry, British writer

What is appropriate in the bedroom? The answer is not the same for all, based on beliefs and values. Some people are more passionate than others. It is a good thing to set boundaries and limitations, and talk about them, to accomplish successful lovemaking. Just saying, "I love you" throughout each encounter is good, but it is not good enough. Successful lovemaking is not always easy, especially if one partner needs more attention than the other. Deal with each other openly and honestly.

Adult sex toys are offensive to some and satisfactory for others. If adult movies are offensive to one, then the sexual relationship may have issues. Ask the serious questions, like, "Will this be physically or psychologically abusive? Will there be a sense of respect for each other after the lovemaking? What will this do to contribute to the total picture of love, a love that is more than sex?"

Making love is a beautiful God given creation, and should be included in the realm of the spiritual as well. Making love is not sinful and should be appreciated and cherished. One can find spiritual moments in making love when true love is the motivation.

True love is not arrogant. Human sexuality runs the risk of arrogance when a partner attempts to dominate the other in the bedroom. The Harvard MBA is wrong if the bedroom and the boardroom are two sides of the same ball game. Using sex to dominate, manipulate, or agitate leads to a destructive ending. The rules in the boardroom are not the same rules in the bedroom. If Ann Landers is correct that divorce starts in the bedroom, then the boardroom cannot be the same. The only good analogy, referring to the bedroom and boardroom, is a baseball analogy noting that both are trying to hit home runs out of the ballpark! But that is not going to happen every time.

The English playwright, Alan Ayckbourn, wrote, "My mother used to say... if sex ever raises its ugly head, close your eyes before you see the rest of it." The ugliness of sex has some roots in religious history. However, fear of sexually transmitted diseases is a real concern, and there is reason not to throw caution to the wind. Religion has also helped with the message in this area of concern. Fear is also connected to a spouse's concern when there is a lack of sex in the relationship. The diminishing of sexual contact leads to the insecurity of a spouse. Several serious cracks in a marital relationship occur when sexuality begins to fade.

The Swiss psychiatrist, Carl Jung, once commented, "First it was passion, then it became duty, and finally an intolerable burden." Such is the sex act when love is not primary in the relationship. Sex without love is "hollow." And, love without sex is "ridiculous." The common denominator for all sex acts is love, especially when love is not envious, arrogant, or rude.

KEEPING LOVE

"He ploughed her, and she cropped."

SHAKESPEARE, ANTHONY AND CLEOPATRA

"Sex is like money; only too much is enough."

JOHN UPDIKE, AMERICAN NOVELIST

"Women complain about sex more than men. Their gripes fall into two major categories: (1) Not enough, (2) Too much."

ANONYMOUS

Rude and crude could be linked together. Love is neither. The rudeness and crudeness sometimes evolves into physical, emotional, and mental abuse. If anyone is facing this challenge each day with a partner, the abuser needs to seek help immediately and if the abuser refuses, then the abused needs to remove himself or herself from the situation. No one is required to remain in an abusive relationship. Counseling is suggested at all costs. Too many people go to counselors after the marriage has been broken. Preventive counseling is an effective approach.

Marriage enrichment programs are beneficial as preventive counseling.

The temptation of infidelity is heightened when the sexual relationship is tied to selfish needs relating to insensitive rude language, crude acts of violence, and careless actions of psychological and mental abuse. Individuals become more vulnerable when sexual relations at home become totally dysfunctional. The result of infidelity, too often, takes partnership from the frying pan to the fire.

Preserving love may require the most honest expression of feelings an individual can muster up in a partnership. Discussing and communicating sexual failures is not easy. The question is straight and forward, do you really and truly want a whole and total love to exist in the marriage? Marriage is a great institution, but it is not the institution to be put in to correct mental and psychological problems without, and often, destroying the other partner. Drug addition, for example, contributes to mental and marital destruction.

Such addictions tend to destroy love that otherwise could bear the fruits of a good and lasting relationship.

The following is referred to as Ten Commandments of Human Sexuality. These are assembled from my twenty-five years of personal experience in counseling, teaching, and studying. Most of these relate to actual comments made to me in marital counseling.

I

THOU SHALL KNOT IF YOU DO NOT FOCUS ON PERFORMANCE.

II

THOU SHALL KNOT IF YOU DO NOT VIEW SEXUALITY AS A DUTY.

III

THOU SHALL KNOT IF YOU DO NOT USE SEXUALITY AS RELEASE OF PERSONAL FRUSTRATIONS.

IV

THOU SHALL KNOT IF YOU DO NOT USE SEXUALITY FOR DECEPTION

V

THOU SHALL KNOT IF YOU DO NOT USE SEXUALITY TO DEMONSTRATE PHYSICAL POWER AND CONTROL.

VI

THOU SHALL KNOT IF YOU DO NOT USE SEXUALITY TO REPLACE VERBAL COMMUNICATION

VII
THOU SHALL KNOT IF YOU DO NOT PLACE SEXUALITY ON THE CALENDER. TRUST SPONTANEITY.

VIII
THOU SHALL KNOT IF YOU ARE NOT INSENSITIVE TO A PARTNER'S PERSONAL NEEDS. DISCUSS MUCH.

IX
THOU SHALL KNOT IF YOU DO NOT USE SEX FOR PURPOSES OF REVENGE.

X
THOU SHALL KNOT IF YOU DO NOT NEGLECT SAFE SEX IN THE PARTNERSHIP.

The practice of these commandments will aid in tying the knot in romance and in respect for sexual encounters of the best kind. Each one helps to touch our inner feelings and helps to express our true selves. Following these commandments will open the door of honesty. This will, in turn, bring results of true love. True love is enhanced through human sexuality.

When performance becomes the focus, then pressure takes over at times and diminishes the enjoyment. Usually with a focus only on performance, enough is never enough, leading to a possible use of physically damaging responses. There may be a need to "top" the last one. In the long run performance will become less satisfactory.

If duty is the reason for human sexuality with your loved one, then love has failed. Duty is without true feelings and becomes dishonest in time. Duty breeds routine. A routine does not bring satisfaction and compassion is often lost.

Using human sexuality for the release of our personal frustrations is a very selfish action. Selfishness is rude and destroys the concept of holiness and wholeness in sex. Both are needed in a successful relationship.

Deception, as a reason for making love, eliminates trust. After awhile the "trick" will not pay off. One partner may appear a little smarter than the other. On the other hand, a partner may not be so dumb, but trusts because of being in love. That is a very deep love, and once wounded may be the end of the relationship.

If human sexuality becomes a power and dominance game, then the game will be tilted. This could be the beginning of physical abuse. Abusive sex diminishes self-respect and self-esteem. Dominance is a sickness that desperately needs counseling as soon as possible. Reconciliation is difficult once the "game" gets out of control.

When making love calls for communication, then communicate. Discussion before or after an uneventful event helps the future of the relationship to be more positive. Partners only put off the inevitable, and the inevitable may be more unpleasant in the long run.

Spontaneity creates some of the most enjoyable sexual relations. Calendars are for dates. Sexuality is for recreation as well as procreation. Serendipity lights sexual fires that increase the excitement so rewarding for the lasting relationship. Keeping the lovemaking in marriage is orchestrated by the music of spontaneity.

There are simply times when a partner really does not feel in the mood. It may be physical or psychological. No matter, discuss it. Insensitivity ruins the partnership and sexuality becomes demeaning. Now if a partner has had a headache for three years every time there is a need to make love, well, discuss much and seek help!

Revenge is childish. Using sex to get even with a spouse is, perhaps, one of the low points in a marriage. A decision to not have sex because a spouse did not have his or her way on some other point of reference represents the beginning of the end. Some serious counseling is suggested. Revenge becomes hatred and hatred is not love. Revenge is rudeness, crudeness, and childish. Whatever it is, it is not love.

Safe sex is no joke. Many mistakes have been made when unmarried partners believe they are immune from sexual diseases. This denial is very prevalent among the elderly. They may have had a life-long partner die, and now they find themselves in an assisted facility. Loneliness is a major occurrence and sexual activity is a reality, whether some people want to accept it or not. Safe sex is not practiced and the results are devastating. Condoms are not just for preventing pregnancy. Multiple partners are not recommended, but if practiced, then safe sex should not be ignored. Safe sex is not to be taken lightly if one is very serious about maintaining good health.

These commandments are not all inclusive, but they certainly represent a wake-up call to evaluate sexual relationships. If love is to be kept in the marriage, then some very positive prevention methods are acceptable. Everything that can be done to keep love in the relationship should be explored.

SUMMARY

Human sexuality shall not be separated from love. Trust is a major factor in connecting love to sexual relationships. Dealing openly and honestly with problems relating sexuality keeps love in focus.

Making love is a beautiful art, created by the Creator of life, for recreation and procreation. A strong faith shared by partners enhances the spiritual moments in love relationships. When sexuality begins to fade in a marriage, counseling should be seriously considered. If the marriage is worthwhile, then partners don't just run away. Seek help before the relationship is completely broken.

The Ten Commandments of Human Sexuality assist partners in avoiding a devastating sex life. These commandments encourage partners to look beyond the routine of making love. Selfishness is overcome and trust is established through practicing these commandments. Abusiveness is not allowed and manipulation is rejected. Such commandments do not allow sex to replace communication. Discussion of individual feelings about sexual needs is encouraged. The commandments promote spontaneity and foster the relationships needed to remember the times for safe sex. Sex should not be used for revenge. The Ten Commandments of Human Sexuality helps us to keep romance in the relationship. True love is never envious, arrogant, or rude.

DISCUSSION QUESTIONS

FOOLING AROUND

Loving

1. What is your understanding of a whole and realistic love?
2. How can dominance diminish the love in a healthy marriage?
3. What happens when love and sexuality are separated in a relationship?
4. In what way does whole love keep a marriage free of arrogance?
5. What is intimacy when sexuality is not included?

Making Love

1. Are you comfortable in discussing your sexuality with your partner?
2. Do you have a problem with believing sex is for recreation and procreation?
3. Do you believe sex is sinful?
4. What do you do when sex has been lost in a marriage?
5. How do you deal with the fear of a marriage falling apart?

Keeping Love

1. Are you willing to seek counseling when a marriage is in trouble?
2. Do you believe in preventive marital issues before the marriage is stale?
3. What makes for a worthwhile marriage?
4. How would your religious faith be primary in reconciling a marriage?
5. How can the Ten Commandments of Human Sexuality contribute to a successful marriage?

LOVE DOES NOT INSIST ON ITS OWN WAY; IT IS NOT IRRITABLE OR RESENTFUL

4

Fighting

"Breathes there a man with soul so dead, who never to his wife hath said, Breakfast be damned, come back to bed."
ANONYMOUS

QUARRELS

A pastor called on two church members, a husband and wife. Seeking to impress the minister with piety, they recounted the blessings of their marriage. The husband said, "My wife and I have lived together for nearly thirty years without a single quarrel."

Such a statement was just too much for the feisty and wise clergyman. He thumped his walking cane on the floor and responded, "Terribly monotonous, man, terribly monotonous."

A married couple claiming no arguments, no disagreements, or quarrels must live a thousand miles apart! Their souls must be so dead that they are totally void of emotions. Human relationships seldom grow without some conflict. Conflict can be healthy and might keep emotions high enough to say, "Breakfast be damned, come back to bed." Conflict is healthier if the partners can learn some lessons of life within the marriage.

Emotions are not easily turned on or off like a faucet. Thinking of the definition, "It (love) does not insist on its own way", requests that emotions be controlled. There should be some ground rules for fighting. Ground rules can control the heat of emotions that can get very ugly. The movie, *War of Roses*, may be exaggerated in the minds of some people, but there are, and have been, marriages that equate to that type of violence. Physical or mental abuse reaches past the boundaries of effective quarreling.

Try to achieve reconciliation before going to bed. This rule is aged, but effective. Going to sleep while angered results in a sleepless night, and the next day the problem usually heightens if left unattended the night before.

Avoid verbal abuse. Abusive words will "kill" the spirit. Words can be spoken that cannot be easily taken back without leaving a wound so deep that the scar will be a constant reminder of the quarrel. Remember the thought, "Speak sweet words because you may have to eat them!"

Domestic violence is a major problem and must not be ignored. After four years of crisis counseling I witnessed the results of domestic violence and realize the dire straits in which some partners find themselves. Usually economic limitations force a partner to remain in a dangerous situation, but there are places and homes available for help. Domestic violence is not related to normal marital conflicts, arguments, or a lover's quarrel. My experience concludes that domestic violence occurs in more than twenty-five percent of marriages.

Physical abuse includes shoving, pushing, restraining, hitting, or kicking. More women are physically battered than men. However, a small percentage of men are battered. Trust your basic instincts and find help. Find someone that can be trusted because physical abuse should not be tolerated.

Another ground rule to remember is to express feelings as quickly as possible. Keeping emotions bottled up inside will eventually create an emotional time bomb ready to explode at any moment. Ill feelings accumulate like a boil that will fester and burst. It is not pretty. Actually, it is very ugly. When both partners expect a quick response then surprises will be minimal. Discussion of rules is helpful. Love does not insist on its own way.

DEFENSES

Fragile emotions require some defenses. For example, don't walk away. Walking away only creates further problems. Leaving the house with the hope everything will be okay when returning, is living in the Land of Oz. Arguments are best served when both couples remain and work through the situation. Solutions come when partners work together through the problems from beginning to end.

When did the argument begin? What pushed the anger buttons? How can the differences be comprised? Is the argument so bad that kissing and making up is not considered as a solution? Mature people will discuss the solutions when the heat of the moment dies a bit because love does not have its own way.

Evaluate the defenses established within the relationship. Is the goal to simply to place blame on one or the other? Is the same partner taking the blame every time? Who is willing to buy ownership into the quarrel? Consistent and continued blame eventually leads to desperation within the marriage. Responsibility should set a goal of mutual understanding.

Is there yelling? Is the defense system to see who can yell the loudest? Does screaming really drown out the argument or provide solutions? Another responsibility is to establish an atmosphere of reasoning. Elevated anger, demonstrated through voice volume, eliminates the opportunity for logical understanding. Emotions tend to overshadow reasoning when left without controls.

Does throwing things endanger the situation? Some say, "Well, I don't throw anything directly at my partner." That is not a positive mode of thinking.

Throwing objects indicates the defense system has been shattered, or indicates a defense system is badly needed. Practicing how to duck is not the answer!

"The course of true love never did run smooth." Shakespeare: *A Midsummer-Night's Dream.* Truer words have never been spoken. If utopia in marriage is expected, then disappointment will be more than a little devastating. Too many couples enter a binding relationship with expectations so unreasonable that when the sexuality begins to fade, the spirit of the relationship is lost. It is not uncommon at this point for quarrels to escalate. Tensions run rather high when the physical attraction has run its course. Dealing with this concern often leads to impulsive anger that appears to be without reason, but in truth, anger is subconsciously preparing to explode.

The realization that marriage is a work in progress from inception to eternity is a positive step. Quarrels are a fact of relationships that follow a typical pattern of forming, storming, and performing. Moving through the process does not mean the process ends when the stage of performing concludes. The process may be repeated at any time. The key is that the storming is less often and less intense. This is a sign of maturity in the relationship. An anonymous author makes a lot of sense: "Love rules without a sword, Love binds without a cord."

MERCIES

Forgiveness is at the heart of reconciliation. Love and forgiveness are in the same category of Christian grace. Hearing the words, "I'm sorry" goes a long way in healing the pains of arguments. Accepting forgiveness brings hope, peace, and the restoration of love. Grace is forgiveness. In the book, Love Story, "Love is never having to say you are sorry." Such naïve thinking could only end up in a Hollywood movie!

Forgiveness sometimes comes with a price tag. It can be costly and painful to forgive. Pride and ego get in the way. There is a teaching that forgiving and forgetting are required. Forgetting is not done or required, only forgiveness. The line to "forgive and forget" is from Shakespeare's *King Lear.* That is so much easier said then done.

During counseling an embittered wife said to me that she might be able to forgive, but she would never be able to forget her husband's affair with another woman. She cried, "The pain is so deep I will never forget his unfaithfulness." This a price tag one often pays after forgiveness, the pain of never forgetting. Some have called it a cross to bear. Wounds will leave scars, but such is the price of mercy. Such mercy is the gift of love.

Forgiveness is sometimes a process. Forgiveness may be a journey that takes a long road to recovery. Mercies do not come easy for some partners. A strong faith will contribute to successful recoveries because love is the aim of such a faith. Christian teachings direct people to the right road on which to take the journey. Personalities are so different and emotions are so controlling that time is the dictator of final results.

Mercy is a quality of maturity and sets the stage for a sustaining foundation on which to build love. Marriage may be made in heaven, but it has to be worked out on earth. Spiritual moments occur when forgiveness reigns supreme. Repairing the broken elements of a relationship provides open doors to the minds and hearts of lovers. Mercies do reign

Shakespeare's words, on the subject of mercy, help to complete relationships when put into practice:

> *"The quality of mercy is not strained,*
> *It droppeth as the gentle dew from heaven*
> *Upon the place beneath; it is twice blessed;*
> *It blesseth him that gives and him that takes;*
> *'Tis mightiest in the mightiest; it becomes*
> *The throned monarch better than his crown."*

SUMMARY

Couples who claim they never argue, quarrel, or fight must live a thousand miles apart! There are ground rules for disagreements, and both parties should have input into establishing these ground rules.

Do defenses assist in settling arguments? How? Is the same person always blamed in an argument? Is there yelling? Are objects thrown? Who is willing to say, "I'm sorry?"

Forgiveness is at the heart of reconciliation. Forgiveness comes with a price. Forgiveness has healing powers. Forgiveness is often a process and not necessarily a singular event. Mercy blesses those who give, as well as blessing the receiver.

DISCUSSION QUESTIONS

FIGHTING

Quarrels

1. Is there a pattern to be found in the quarreling between partners?
2. Do you have ground rules for fighting in your marriage?
3. Does your relationship identify with the ground rules in this chapter?
4. Do you disagree with laying ground rules?
5. What does one NOT do in relation to domestic abuse?

Defenses

1. What are your defenses when engaged in marital disagreements?
2. What would be your definition of a mature relationship?
3. Does your relationship identify with the defenses in this chapter?
4. What do you think your individual responsibilities are in a marital argument?
5. Have you discussed the possibility of premarital or marital counseling?

Mercies

1. What is at the heart of reconciliation?
2. What is the price tag on forgiveness?
3. Why is forgiveness a healing power?
4. Why is forgiveness more of a process than a singular event?
5. How would you relate mercy to maturity?

LOVE DOES NOT REJOICE IN WRONGDOING, BUT REJOICES IN THE TRUTH

5

FIDELITY

"I have looked on a lot of women with lust.
I have committed adultery in my heart many times.
This is something God recognizes I will do ...and God forgives me for it."
JIMMY CARTER, PRESIDENT OF THE UNITED STATES, (1976 PLAYBOY INTERVIEW.)

"I did it because I could."
WILLIAM JEFFERSON CLINTON, PRESIDENT OF THE UNITED STATES,
(ANSWERING A QUESTION RELATING TO THE MONICA LEWINSKY AFFAIR.)

TROUBLE

Suspicions will dramatically destroy the very best of relationships. There is a story relating to the biblical characters of Adam and Eve. The story goes that Adam was staying out late for several nights in a row. Eve became suspicious, and rightly so. Terribly upset she charged, "You are running around with other women."

Adam responded, "You are unreasonable. You are the only woman on earth for me!"

The argument continued into the late night until Adam finally fell asleep. During sleep Adam awoke with a poking in the chest. It was Eve. "What do you think you are doing?" Adam demanded.

"I'm counting your ribs." Eve said.

Yes, there was trouble in the Garden of Eden. There is trouble in every marriage when one spouse is constantly suspicious of the other. Assumptions are not solutions to suspicions. Suspicions breed distrust and doubt, and then truth is lost.

Say what you mean and mean what you say. Get everything out into the open. Holding back with a few verbal jabs here and there accomplishes nothing but a big emotional explosion in the end. The key is in telling the truth. There are situations in which the truth must be defined. Some will argue the truth is the truth. How can one define the truth?

TRUTH

> *"You want to be very careful about lying, otherwise you are nearly sure to get caught."*
>
> MARK TWAIN, (SAMUEL CLEMONS), AMERICAN WRITER, LECTURER

> *"The punishment of the liar is that he eventually believes his own lies."*
>
> ELBERT HUBBARD, AMERICAN WRITER, PUBLISHER, AND HUMORIST

Lying is dying, most of the time. Death comes to a relationship when lies control the behavior of either spouse. Habitual lying is a sickness. Lies often become easier the more they are told, and the more likely is one to be caught. Until a line of truth is drawn, lying is the internal bomb that eventually implodes the marriage.

Making excuses for lying simply becomes rationalization for one's poor behavior. "Little white lies" are sometimes justified, but only lead to bigger lies when needed. Why is the truth so difficult? The difficulty of truth is that it bares our souls and exposes weakness; therefore it is "easier" to lie.

Infidelity is the one area that frequents lies. Fidelity prevents the need for lying. Temptation will happen for most people at some time in a relationship. Lust occurs from natural instincts and promotes selfishness. Discussing the feelings with a spouse relating to temptations and lust helps to prevent eventual infidelity. Truth is the key to the prevention of infidelity.

Truth opens the emotional doors and allows the real self to be seen. This is scary and defines our vulnerable position in a relationship with another. Love is the risk of being vulnerable. Love rejoices in the truth, not in doing wrong. Truth is worthy of one's personality to be free from dishonesty, deception, and distrust. Allowing someone into the deepest parts of the heart, mind, and soul is fearful, but the process, if given time, will result in the best reward, trust.

TRUST

Trust is the solid foundation in a marriage. Trust comes from rejoicing in the truth. Trust sustains a relationship through the thick and thin, good and bad, rough and tough times that eventually come to any relationship. When practiced trust can bring couples closer through the years. Trust is the cement of a successful marriage. Trust is foremost in providing a total peace of mind. Peace of mind is wealth worth possessing. Infidelity quickly destroys trust and lying adds fuel to the fire.

When infidelity occurs, and the spouse responsible wishes to end the affair, should that spouse tell the truth about the affair? Yes. However, to whom should the guilty party tell the truth? If the truth is told to the partner, the trust level is very seldom ever reestablished to the point of previous harmony. Guilt is usually the guide to tell the truth in order to relieve personal pain. But what pain is created for the partner? If the guilty party truly wants to end the affair, and does so permanently, the truth might be told in private counseling. The counselor helps set up boundaries to prevent future infidelities. So, another characteristic of truth, is telling the truth to someone trustworthy and helpful in finding solutions to prevent further infidelities. Some will disagree, but experience in counseling indicates the difficulty to reestablish trust is more than most individuals can handle alone.

The heart cannot easily cradle sin if one has a set of values. Sin will not be long in taking the form of a crisis of conscience. Rejoicing in the truth will challenge sin. The sin of infidelity destroys all that a relationship has built over time.

Then there is the fear of contracting social diseases and passing diseases to the partner. Such fear should be a deterrent to infidelity, but often it is not. On the other hand, fear is not the best motivation to prevent infidelity. Love is the best motivation, even though fear is the strongest emotion. Love is a more sustaining force because love is the pure of the two emotions. Love, not fear, produces genuine trust.

By practicing fidelity marriage will become a haven (heaven) of safety, truth, and trust. Practicing infidelity will become a hell for fear, lies, and deception. The choices and the rewards are clear. The right choices lead to the rewards, and the right choices are not always easy without the understanding and the feeling of love that does not rejoice in wrongdoing, but rejoices in the truth.

SUMMARY

Constant suspicions of one spouse spells big trouble. When suspicions emerge it is time to take some serious steps to repair the broken lines. Certainly, prevention is more positive and provides barriers that keep suspicions out.

Lying is dying. A "little white lie" is seldom successful in achieving its purpose. Truth is the real answer. Truth does expose our vulnerable selves in a way that is scary, but in the long run truth builds the trust marriages need to survive in this imperfect and challenging world.

Who does one tell when infidelity creeps into a relationship? Does a faith value help to guide and direct the conscience? Infidelity is a liability and destroys trust to the point that reestablishing trust comes close to impossible. The truth is always the right choice. Truth defines love at the highest level. "Love does not rejoice in wrongdoing, but rejoices in the truth."

DISCUSSION QUESTIONS

FIDELITY

Trouble

1. Do you have an Adam and Eve story in your married life?
2. What is the major problem with suspicions and assumptions?
3. How do you perceive a matter of truth?
4. How is trust built in a relationship?
5. What is a concern in losing trust?

Truth

1. What position do you take on lying?
2. Is there ever a time for "little white lies" in a marriage?
3. Do you see a way couples might overcome infidelity in a marriage?
4. Can you think of more than one understanding or definition of truth?
5. What do you think is the best reward in a marriage?

Trust

1. How is trust the foundation of a successful relationship?
2. What do you think is the strongest emotion in a marriage?
3. What role does fear play in a relationship?
4. When does marriage enter a safe haven?
5. What is hell in a marriage?

LOVE BEARS ALL THINGS

6

FINANCE

"Keep the fraction constant..."
THEODORE ROOSEVELT, SR.

CAUTION

The father of President Theodore Roosevelt taught his son "fraction" economics. That is, one should keep the numerator larger than the denominator. In plain English, the expenditures should not exceed the income.

Finances have quickly moved to the forefront of issues relating to a happy and sustaining marriage. When the numerator cannot be increased, then the denominator must be decreased. In marriages the struggle is often during a change of numerators. Two incomes are often needed in today's economy, and how these incomes are agreed on and used becomes a test of the relationship. Studies indicate that two checkbooks, two bathrooms, and one bed are good economic and romantic guidelines. One income should not be "mine" and the other "ours."

Separate checking accounts are recommended. Each spouse needs the freedom of managing and appropriating funds. Discussions should be common when large purchases are made that involve both incomes. An agreement should be reached as to the amount that qualifies as a large amount.

"Love bears all things" with an emphasis on "all", bears out the inclusion of finances as an issue in relationships. Financial disputes in marriages are so prone to emotional damage that it must be included in the love that bears all. A careful and deliberate plan to making, saving, and spending money can create a very happy marital atmosphere. The opposite, of course, leads to a cloudy atmosphere at best.

CREDIT

"Never run into debt, not if you can find anything else to run into."
JOSH BILLINGS, AMERICAN WRITER AND HUMORIST

Living from paycheck to paycheck is a haunting way to live. Haunting in the sense that couples never feel relaxed enough to enjoy life, but continually feel the bill collectors are haunting them. Impulsive spending, take it from one who knows, is detrimental to trying to stay on a budget. Family budgets are good when couples can agree on what is important and what is not so necessary. Is there anything that can be left out of living expenses without eliminating the necessities? Spending habits that are not constructive to the marriage need to be challenged with serious counseling assistance.

Paycheck to paycheck opens the door to the dangerous credit. There is good and responsible credit, but under the forces of bill collectors, credit may not be a way out of the financial difficulties. Using credit cards to pay off credit cards on a monthly basis is a caution flag not to be ignored. The world's greatest comic is called "easy payments."

When partners find themselves in financial despair, panic sets in, and the true character of a person is revealed. In despair beware of credit repair. There are legitimate credit helpers, but too often the vulnerable fall into scams and other economic traps. Avoid those who want excessive amounts of money to help with credit problems.

Four men were talking about the greatest invention in the world. One believed the greatest invention was the train. Another declared the automobile was the greatest invention. Still another believed the airplane qualified. The fourth man had been silent, and then he finally said, "The one who started credit was no bum, because interest is the greatest invention."

High interest rates may not be in our best interest. One basic rule for borrowing money is NOT! However, there are times when borrowing is necessary and prudent. Some serious questions may be in order before making the credit decision. These questions are forged from counseling experiences that others have found beneficial.

1. What is your purpose for borrowing?
2. How much will the money cost? (Interest Rate)
3. Can you live without the items or services?
4. Will this spending jeopardize future financial goals?
5. When is the timing for necessary borrowing appropriate?

What is the purpose for borrowing the money? Home improvement makes more sense than borrowing for vacations or gifts for Christmas.

Wife: "Remember our vacation?"

Husband: "Yes, of course I do."

Wife: "Remember how we spent money like there was no tomorrow?"

Husband: "I believe I do."

Wife: "Well, tomorrow has come."

Recognize your situation? Been there, done that, and have the T-shirt?

How much will the money cost? Interest rates vary and research is a good thing. On the other hand, out of desperation, it is tempting to borrow money at any cost. Life insurance polices are sometimes a better deal. Some people turn to equity in their homes. One positive thought rests with family members who are willing to help. Explaining the truth of the financial situation to a family member, with the idea that they may NOT get their money back, or it may be a very long time before they get reimbursed, is suggested if this is a last resort. Many families have had hard feelings when the money is not returned, but being up front helps relieve potential family disagreements.

Can you live without the items or services? Most of the time it is possible to do without things that are not basic. The basics are food, shelter, and clothing. Outside of the basics one must determine what is most important. Department stores and other commercial businesses count on impulsive spending. (By the way, so-called discount outlets are NOT always the best deals.) Impulsive spending leaves out the opportunity to discuss big ticket items. Impulsive spending is often the root of poor money management, and too often leads to the valley of despair.

Where else but in America do so many people drive bank financed automobiles, down bond-financed highways, using credit cards for gasoline? Too often the credit crunch leads to credit disaster, and the need to openly and honestly deal with the problem will help partners bear all things. Love does work out some of the most difficult financial concerns when people who love one another work with the same goals in mind.

Will this spending jeopardize future financial goals? An unfortunate businessman spent his entire adult life declaring and recovering from bankruptcy. After his death a note was discovered requesting his pallbearers be six bankers who had been a major part of his adult years. It read, "These gentleman carried me all my life. Let them finish the job!"

Death may come quicker if our lives are consistently attacked by the emotional strain of paying the bankers. Future goals like planning for retirement may be placed in jeopardy when foolish spending and poor budget planning is ignored. A close friend once said, "John, you can't have too much money for retirement." Social Security was meant to be a supplement to retirement and not "the" retirement income. Therefore, married couples often find themselves having to choose between medicine and food.

This is destructive to the relationship and often creates callous feelings between the partners. So many people are now living to the age of one hundred, and that will tax the budget planning for the future. Couples cannot save too much, or start too soon in the saving process.

When is the timing for necessary borrowing appropriate? As some have heard, "Timing is everything." Getting a good mortgage rate on a home is related to good timing. Many couples need cars in relation to their professions. When is the best time to purchase? Credit cards are necessary when booking airline flights, vacations, and motel rooms, to name a few. A number of options exist with cards of different interest rates. Knowing present interest rates on cards helps with the timing. Research is the answer to many timing situations for the best credit value.

The primary problem with borrowing money is that money must be repaid, often with interest! Borrowing money is a lot easier than paying the debt. Some credit cards could take years to pay off the minimum balance if this is the only goal of repayment. Paying off debts can hurt more than the checkbook, and even more importantly, the marriage.

CHARITY

John Wesley, credited with founding what is known today as The United Methodist Church, had some very clear thoughts regarding money and the use of money. The governing principle of Wesley's teaching on the use of money is that money exists for humans and not that humans exist for money. He noted, "Money is unspeakably precious, if we are wise and faithful stewards of it." Thus, charity plays a major role in Wesley's use of money. In his sermon, *The Use of Money,* his philosophy of charity was evident. Simply put: "Gain all you can. Save all you can. Give all you can." He demonstrated his belief by giving away most everything he earned.

So, in marriage, what is the philosophy of giving? Each couple makes the decision, but not without discussion. Some people have been so caught up in a church's demand for giving that they have gone bankrupt. Partners need to make reasonable charity decisions based on religious or secular moral values, or what really makes sense. Giving is very rewarding for a number of people, but should never become a divisive factor in the relationship.

There is a saying, "When it comes to giving, some people stop at NOTHING." Nothing should be out of the question in a martial relationship. Especially where children are involved, charity goes a long way in teaching the value of giving for the children. Charity is a demonstration of love. Love can bear all.

SUMMARY

Financial strain ranks at the top in the causes of failed marriages. Discussions about money should be mandatory in the purchase of large ticket items. In marriage, as in most of life, money can become a love or hate factor. Is your denominator larger than your numerator?

Impulsive spending is an addiction, and is often a contributing factor in poor spending habits. Poor budget planning also lends to negative money management.

What is the purpose for spending? Can you live without the purchase?

Charity is love and love bears all. Are you prepared to give all you can? The call to share our possessions relates to the word "communion" and means to care and share.

DISCUSSION QUESTIONS

FINANCE

Caution

1. What do you think about the statement: "All income should be ours?"
2. Do you believe in separate checking accounts?
3. If your answer is no, why?
4. What is your understanding about money, a hate or love factor?
5. What is your feeling about "fraction economics"?

Credit

1. What do you think should be a basic rule for borrowing money?
2. When common sense meets impulsive spending, how do you cope?
3. How would you approach "timing" when it comes to spending?
4. Do you really need credit cards or will one card suffice?
5. What are your plans for retirement?

Charity

1. What is your opinion of John Wesley's philosophy about money?
2. Do you believe that the love of money is the root of evil?
3. How can wealth diminish morals and values?
4. How does poverty diminish morals and values?
5. Are you willing to discuss charity as a part of your budget planning?

LOVE BELIEVES ALL THINGS

7

FRIENDSHIP

"I fanned the flame of friendship and it fired love."
ALEXANDER DREY

"A friend is one who comes in when the whole world goes out."
EDGAR DEWITT JONES

"Laughter is not a bad beginning for friendship..."
OSCAR WILDE

HALLMARK OF FRIENDSHIP

Many a love began with friendship. Countless couples communicate to me during premarital counseling they had a good friendship before they became lovers. Some indicate their friendship was a gradual process. Others believe their friendship came after the marriage and has made their marriage stronger. Maybe George Washington was more than just a President. He said, "True friendship is a plant of slow growth."

A slow growing friendship may be extremely healthy in the long-term stability of a marriage. Friendship often flows from planted seeds, like love, honor, and respect. In the context of "Love believes all things", friendship stabilizes the hurts and pains of life within a partnership because most people need someone to believe in them when others do not. Life throws curve balls with such a resounding negative effect that a person can be left devastated without the feeling of security. In other words, love is friendship and believes in all things, thus providing a needed security.

Love can be fired in friendship. Aristotle was asked the definition of a friend, and he replied, "A single soul which dwells in two bodies." The hallmark of friendship is when partners believe they are soul-mates. There are many definitions of a soul-mate, but the definition that does not include friendship is void of a complete understanding of relationships. There is no situation that occurs in the relationship that cannot find solace when spouses stand by each other, and especially when the world appears to be against them. Standing together creates a binding cord of supreme strength that will not allow anything to bring down the relationship.

What is a friend? "A friend is a person who shares all your glad times, laughs with you, cries with you, helps you through the sad times..." (Excerpts from a Hallmark Card)

Note the word "all." If love is to believe "all" things and friendship includes sharing "all", then marriage is as close to anything in providing the context in which "all" will occur. Marriage, then, requests the understanding of the "all" inclusive definition.

After being thanked by a friend for a good deed, have you ever responded with the words, "Well, what are friends for?" The same goes for loving couples. Friendship type responses you expect outside of marriage also apply to the friendship within the marriage. A tremendous feeling of security comes to pass when a love relationship is also treated as a friend relationship.

Friends who can share in laughter find a relief from the ordinary and the extremes in a partnership. A marriage friendship grows with a good sense of humor. Laughter increases the closeness and reduces the tension and trials that occur during the times when the absurd takes over. The absurd includes those times when couples have absolutely no control over the situation. What else can you do but laugh? The hallmark of friendship, say soul-mates, depends a lot on knowing when you need some good laughs.

HOUSE OF FRIENDSHIPS

"Love begets respect and friendship surely follows."

JEAN COCTEAU

All relationships do not develop in the same way. There are no set rules or textbooks that can guide couples to a perfect friendship that exists with romance. However, respect should never be ignored as a major ingredient in the recipes for love and friendship.

Respect becomes a cornerstone for friendship within romance in more ways than one. For example, there are friendships outside the marriage for each of the spouses. Some of these friendships will simply not work for both parties at times. Respect for these separate friendships should be acknowledged. In cases where couples mix with other couples or single friends on a regular basis, spouses need to respect the opportunities to share friends not always acceptable to the other. Compromises become important or arguments persist where routine interpersonal friendships exist.

Mixing friendships becomes a house of friendships and suggests that some guidelines be established. If one partner has known a friend or friends longer than the other partner, the possibility of the partner who is less acquainted may feel left out. This is a true feeling to be concerned about. In a situation where one partner has been divorced, and has friends from the past marriage, should the new spouse be expected to blend right in with his or her old friends? This is a conflict that can be prevented if there is sincere respect for the partner who might be uneasy in the presence of people whom they do not know well as the spouse. If love believes all things, then friendship within the romance must sometimes take a different approach. Friends do not have to be given up, nor do friends have to be forced on a loved one. The solution is not always simple, and the reality is that it is a respectful person who learns ways to prevent problems under these circumstances.

Respect in the house of friendships requires giving and taking. Give and take helps to solve the more tense situations when spouses have disagreements on friendship. Shortchange a friend and one deceives the act of true love. Shortchanging a spouse on his or her needs for other friendships only adds to possible diminishing returns on the success of the marriage.

HEART OF FRIENDSHIP

> *"Friendship bridges the gap between what things are and what they could be."*
>
> ROGER HOLMES

Friendship within the romance helps to open the eyes of blind romance. Romance has a tendency to set us apart from reality when making decisions of importance that affect the individual or both partners. Friendship practiced becomes the eye-opener in a way that helps us make better choices. Friendship enables a person within the marriage to discern what is more practical by keeping us honest about our feelings and decisions. Logic is too often not applied to some situations because romance blinds us. Emotions take over and reasoning is diminished. A person needs a friend within a marriage that can respond, "Now I'm speaking as a friend; think before you act."

Allowing a friendship to exist within a marriage, to the point that reasoning is a challenge to emotions, is the heart of friendship within the marriage. "I am your friend. Please don't let that get in the way of our love." (JHG) This personal quote can help put into perspective the positive combination of romance and friendship.

SUMMARY

"True friendship is a plant of slow growth," wrote George Washington. People within lifetime commitments find love in friendship and friendship in love.

Friendship responses outside of marriage apply also to friendships in marriage. A positive dose of humor is good for a positive friendship within the marriage.

Respect in friendship allows the door to open to a special feeling that requires giving and taking with the emphasis on giving.

Roger Holmes said, "Friendship bridges the gap between what things are and what they could be." These words help us understand that the heart of friendship helps us apply reason in difficult situations that tend to be controlled only by emotions. The context of marriage provides the on-going institution to perfect friendship and romance. What things could be, rather than what they are, helps us to believe all things are possible with friendship and love.

DISCUSSION QUESTIONS

FRIENDSHIP

Hallmark of Friendship

1. What is your definition of friendship?
2. In what ways do you think true friendship is a plant of slow growth?
3. What are some of the seeds of friendship?
4. Would you agree that respect is the primary seed? Why?
5. What is the value of humor in a relationship?

House of Friendship

1. How do romance and friendship find a partnership?
2. Do you believe in sharing your friends with your partner?
3. Do you have friends from a previous relationship that your present partner rejects?
4. What is the difference between a demanding friendship and a giving friendship?
5. What does it mean to shortchange a friendship?

Heart of Friendship

1. Do you believe that friendship helps balance the romance within the marriage?
2. What are some ways to nurture friendship in a marriage?
3. Do love and friendship believe all things are possible?
4. Do you believe friendship within marriage helps discern the best decision making policy?
5. Discuss what might happen if friendship stands in the way of romance.

LOVE HOPES ALL THINGS

8

FUN

*"There is great gaiety in the heart of God,
for many things in the world
appear to be here just for the fun of it..."*

THE REVEREND DR. GENE ZIMMERMAN, RETIRED UNITED METHODIST MINISTER

TIME OUT

The Reverend Dr. Gene Zimmerman, friend and mentor, comments on enjoying life for the fun of it in his book, *Why do Mullet Jump?* Dr. Zimmerman writes, "No one seems to know why mullet jump. My guess is they do it for the same reason children skip, bear cubs tussle, or a young colt suddenly breaks and runs – just for the fun it." Well, as the saying goes, "birds do it, bees do it." Yes, sex is fun too. However, in addition to sex, there is a need for partners to enjoy life for the fun of it.

An eighty-five year old woman, diagnosed with terminal cancer, was asked, "What would you do differently if you could live your life over?"

She responded with confidence, "I would eat more ice cream and less beans."

Taking life less seriously as individuals and couples, insists that more fun improves mental and physical wellness. A need to work and not play is not a virtue.

Early on in marriage fun is not the problem it appears to be in a marriage that moves toward longevity. Couples find themselves in a rut when there is no relief from the routines of daily work and responsibilities. There are some partners who need to plan their fun and there are others who enjoy the spontaneity of the moment. Those who worship on their Sabbath realize Sabbath was not made for the people, but people for the Sabbath. Rest, relaxation, and meditation are times for fun and enjoyment.

A minister became acquainted with a famous professional baseball player. During a conversation the minister said to the player, "Why must you play ball on the Sabbath?"

"Well, Reverend," smiled the player, "Sabbath is our biggest attendance day! And, by the way, the Sabbath is your biggest day, too. Isn't it?"

The minister nodded and added, "But you see I'm in the right field."

The player's face brightened and he eagerly responded, "That's where I play, right field, and ain't it hell out there?"

Whatever day is Sabbath for you, the soul often needs as much rest as the body, and often the two are related. Spiritual rests provides a "hope for all things." If a couple buys into the thought that love hopes all things, then it is possible to buy into the thought that the enjoyment of life brings hope. Hope is rare for so many people and taking time to renew our spirits helps creates a high degree of comfort for the body and peace for the mind.

TIME TOGETHER

Successful partnerships need enjoyment together as well as separately. A date a week is not a bad idea. Vacations that do not reduce the budget to a level of poverty are very helpful. Americans have or take the least amount of time to enjoy vacations than most modern day societies. Money should not be an excuse for not finding enjoyable times away from home. There are creative ways to get away, and not have to worry about paying your mortgage.

Staying home and planning a great time together, or occasional invitations for friends to join the fun, is also possible. Thinking that going away from home is the best way to enjoy a vacation is not necessarily true. Some professions require more time away from home, so staying home for vacationing can be a good deal. Home can be the hope for rest of body and peace of mind. Home is sanctuary for some and a wonderful time to do therapy: clean the car, garage, or work in the yard. Others might think that is a prison sentence. As the saying goes, "Different strokes for different folks."

A couple was approached by a Realtor to sell them a home. "A home?" answered the wife. "We don't need a home. I was born in a hospital, educated in a boarding school, dated in an automobile, married in a church, eat in restaurants, spend time on the golf course, play bridge with friends, and in the evenings people invite us to dinner. All we need is a garage!"

Time together sets the stage for improvement in communication for the family. Communication times are valuable. A cartoon in a popular newspaper years ago had a caption that read: "We don't communicate anymore," complained the wife.

The husband responded, "What do you mean we don't communicate anymore? Didn't you read the memo I left on the kitchen table?"

TIME APART

Separate fun is the way for some partners. Even separate vacations are positive for some marriages. Each person has his or her own idea of fun, and two happily married people might go separate ways to enjoy their favorite hobby, sport, or interest. All people are not interested in NASCAR races and drinking beer as a means of fun.

A friend, who is an artist by profession, seeks time away alone to enjoy the serenity of the woods and all that nature provides for the soul. He enjoys biking in the forests while the wife prefers biking on the beach. "I stop sometimes," he says, "and sit under an oak tree and listen to the acorns fall." His wife, on the other hand, loves the beach and allows the sand to pass through her toes when she is not biking. She enjoys listening to the wind as the gentle breezes brush her face. Her tranquility is enhanced by the sound of the ocean. So each one has a different way to find his or her solace and fun.

A time for fun, relaxation, and enjoyment of life helps people to look forward to a better day. A sense of hope is established, and many couples find married life easier and workloads lighter. Life has more hope when fun reins in the voids of life. Love understands the individual needs. "Love hopes all things."

SUMMARY

"There is a great gaiety in the heart of God for many things in the world appear to be here just for the fun of it." The Reverend Dr. Gene Zimmerman

A couple does not have to spend a lot of money to have fun. A couch potato might be good for some, but not for all. Spontaneity springs forward with adventure. Have a regular date time. Home can be a place of fun. Separate fun times are okay.

DISCUSSION QUESTIONS

FUN

Time Out

1. What do you like to do for fun?
2. What are some creative ways to have fun?
3. Do you take time out for the soul?
4. What are some ways to enjoy spiritual rest?
5. What do you think might be the results of spiritual rest?

Time Together

1. Do you have regular dates in your married life?
2. Do you allow, "too busy today" to interfere with your fun time?
3. How would you define quality time together?
4. What do you do when communication breaks down in a relationship?
5. Do you truly have fun in your present lifestyle?

Time Apart

1. What do you think of separate fun in a marriage?
2. Discuss some of the times you enjoy when having fun with friends.
3. Do you take time to share the differences you have in the enjoyment of life?
4. Do you have a place or places of solitude?
5. What is your most fun thing to do when alone?

LOVE ENDURES ALL

9

FAITH

"Faith makes the discords of the present the harmonies of the future."
ROBERT COLLYER, WRITER

"...the sustenance of courage is faith."
HARRY EMERSON FOSDICK

"A simple childlike faith in a Divine Friend
solves all the problems that come to us by land or sea."
HELEN KELLER

BELIEVING

Married life is a continuous adventure. The adventure of life together, as partners in love for a lifetime, requires the power of a reasonable faith. Faith is not to be viewed as a crutch, but an assurance that the Creator has given us the fortitude to see the best of times during the worst of times.

Partnerships and marriages may fall apart when faith is nothing but wishing. Faith is often a serious development of believing over a period of time. Faith development is an individual and joint process within relationships. Searching for personal and marital faith growth during the summer and spring times of life, sustains couples during the winter times of life. Love tends to endure all when faith provides the courage.

Faith does not necessarily make life easier. Believers may have as many trials and tribulations as doubters. Although the believer experiences broken hearts, setbacks, and multiple crises just like anybody else, courage found through faith is more apt to sustain strength through adversities. Faith is like a seed. Seeds sometime survive the storms of life better than the mighty full-grown tree.

Romanticism has a way of blinding couples to the realities of life and to the true meaning of love. There is an old adage, "When the kissing stops, the cooking keeps on going." Well, in reality, one must eat! In the New Testament scripture teaches that faith, hope, and love exists, but the greatest of these is love. My experience leads me to believe that the strongest of these is faith. Hope and love are built on the foundation of faith. This further directs one to the understanding that faith can replace blinding romanticism and sustain the problems of married life.

BUILDING

> *"Belief or unbelief bears upon life, determines its whole course, begins at its beginning."*
>
> ROBERT BROWNING

Begin where you are and begin with belief. You believe in saving for retirement. You believe in your doctor when you are sick. You believe the meat, vegetables, and liquids you purchase at the grocery store to be safe. You believe in people who work on your automobile to be reliable. You trust people who handle your finances at the bank. In truth, life is built on belief.

Belief is faith. Faith is a building process of learning and believing. In relationships faith building does not arrive without effort. Faith building just might take a lifetime because swimming through the high and low tides of life requires sustained commitment.

During the reconstruction period following World War II, an international meeting was held to determine how the ruined properties, along with the lives of people, might be restored. One person suggested, "We need two "F" words: food and fuel."

Another added, "We need fertilizer as a third "F" word."

And last, someone else contributed a fourth "F" word: faith.

All agreed that without the fourth "F" word all else might become futile.

Building, and sometimes restoring a partnership, suggests many "F" words. The very one that keeps a fair balance in marriage is faith. If one is searching for the "whole" in a positive and lasting relationship, faith can be the foundation for building and restoring. In the Christian teaching Jesus is profound in stating to the person who came for healing, "Your faith has made you whole."

BLESSINGS

When faith plays a major role in married life, blessings do occur. These blessings are not rewards or guarantees for equal satisfaction for all situations. These might be better interpreted as appreciation or gratefulness for surviving or embracing the challenges of life.

In 1998 I was diagnosed with Inclusion Body Myositis. This is the gradual loss of muscle in the biceps and quadriceps. Later on I realized I could no longer run or lift anything of significance. Lifting and exercising my arms has become very painful.

My legs are so weak that on any long trips I must exit from the vehicle every hour or so to massage my legs. The challenge is now combined with tinnitis, a ringing in the ears that creates continual frustration.

The process of reaching the diagnosis is the story of an emotional roller coaster ride. A neurologist suggested in the beginning, not knowing the exact diagnosis, to have a number of tests and examinations. At the time of completing the first series of tests my employer changed insurance companies. The new company required that tests be repeated if they were to pay.

The process to get the approval for new tests took six weeks. New blood tests were then ordered, but the medical clinic lost the capsules of blood. That's all I was told. The second blood test was kept too long at the medical clinic before being mailed for examination, and the blood was too stale for the type of test required. So a third blood test was ordered, but the results were not quite conclusive as to the type of Muscular Dystrophy attacking me. The process for these three blood tests, due to turn around time, took over four weeks. By this time nearly three months had passed since my very first visit to the neurologist.

The neurologist then ordered a muscle biopsy. Sparing the details, the process, including insurance approval, acquiring a date with a doctor who was a specialist in the area, and the turnaround time to get a response from the examination of the muscle portion removed, was another six weeks. The examination revealed that my muscle degeneration was more like that of Inclusion Body Myositis.

Where are my blessings? First, my wife said, "No matter what it takes we will get through this together." Second, friends and family surrounded me with compassion. Third, my faith helped me to face and embrace the challenge before me with a degree of confidence I had not owned in the past. Fourth, I came to realize that it is NOT God's will that biological malfunctions disrupt our lives. Fifth, my eventual conclusion was that it was God's will that I give one hundred percent with the mind and body I have left.

A blessing is not always a physical healing. Sustaining us in the challenges of life within marriage is the blessing. The strength and will to continue in spite of the tragedies is a miracle for me. Once the surrender flag goes up, the blessing is then left in the hands of a Merciful Creator. Death might become the miracle when the pain can no longer be stopped. This miracle is especially true when one has faith in eternal life.

Think of faith in the following manner. Faith can make us whole when faith does not make us physically whole. Faith creates acts of compassion. Faith development moves us to the stage of complete trust in the Divine Friend.

Marriage can function and be whole when there is a shared faith. The world we live in is not always good or fair. God, for my personal faith, is good. In partnerships a marriage can be sustained by sharing a faith in a good God.

SUMMARY

Faith helps to withstand the winter until the spring and summer arrive. Faith produces a sense of strength and courage not known when tragedy strikes. Faith is the assurance that love endures all things in relationships.

Faith does not always make life easier. All things may not be good, but faith can help to make results of life work for good. Refrain from asking "Why?" Rather ask and embrace the question, "What can be done to make my situation better?" This may take time and the development of faith is not always included with express mail.

A shared faith in marriage bonds the cords of the relationship. Faith establishes the willingness and the ability to nurture the seeds of faith. There is a seed of faith in each person that needs to be nurtured.

DISCUSSION QUESTIONS

FAITH

Believing

1. What do you think is the relationship between love and faith?
2. What is the difference between faith and a wish?
3. Explain your feelings about, "Faith does not guarantee to make life easier."
4. Read Romans 8:25: "All things work ..." Discuss the verse.
5. What can a shared faith mean to a married couple?

Building

1. Do you believe doubt is a bad thing?
2. What is the background for your faith?
3. How will your faith, if different, be communicated to your children?
4. Why might worship be important in faith building?
5. Discuss your understanding of faith as a seed.

Blessings

1. What is your definition of a blessing?
2. Share what happened in your relationship in times of illness.
3. Why is it important to share the times of illness?
4. Discuss the marriage vow: "To have and to hold...in sickness or in health."
5. Do you try to communicate your feelings during the trials and tribulations of everyday life?

LOVE NEVER ENDS

10

FUTURE

"A vision foretells what may be ours. It is an invitation to do something.
With a great mental picture in mind we go from one accomplishment to another,
using the materials about us only as steppingstones
to that which is higher and better and more satisfying.
We thus become possessors of the unseen values which are eternal."
KATHERINE LOGAN, WRITER

DISCOVERING VISION

An instructor placed a large sheet of white paper on the classroom wall. She marked a small black dot in the middle of the paper. Then she asked her students to describe what they saw. There were several minutes of uneasy silence. Eventually, one by one, they all had the same answer, "I see a black dot."

The instructor patiently waited, and after several more minutes of the same answer, she said, "That's the problem, you all see a black dot, but none of you see the white paper."

If love is to never end, then partnerships need a broad vision of their future together. Planning for a marital future includes discovering a vision. If couples refuse to see beyond the black dot, then a marriage might become an affair NOT to remember.

Discovering a vision in partnerships generally takes two routes: individual vision and dual vision. Discovering individual vision may be continuing education, position promotion, professional achievements, and establishing positive self-esteem. Questions should arise from a personal vision. Will my continuing education benefit the relationship overall, like better income? Will my promotion include having to move to a different location? How will that affect my spouse's profession? Will my professional achievements take away too much time from quality family time?

Discovering vision working together in a partnership requires asking similar questions to those previously mentioned, plus looking way beyond individual concerns. Discovering vision as a married couple may include children. How will personal vision affect the newborn lives? Since finances are generally the main contribution to failed relationships, what is the financial vision for the future? Are you planning to buy, rent, or live with parents? These are simply practical questions, and represent only a few from the thought giving process that needs to be applied in discovering vision.

A faithful father, seeking to teach his son an example of wisdom, took an apple and split it into two parts. He asked his son, holding up one half of the apple, "What do you see?"

The son answered, "Apple seeds."

His father drove home the point when he said, "Son, you see seeds, I want to teach you to see that the result of the seeds is a mighty apple tree."

Looking beyond today in a marital like relationship, gives a couple the ability to accept tomorrow with a greater degree of assurance. When children enter the picture the pattern of living shifts dramatically. Looking ahead pays off big dividends financially, emotionally, and psychologically.

Since life is progression, it can be comprehended in "becoming." A sense of the future makes sense of life. "Becoming" together helps bond a relationship that will continue to endure no matter what the situation. The situation to come presents fear of the unknown.

Fear can be a major obstacle in the success of a long time relationship looking to the future. Fear, the strongest of emotions, can hold back meaningful partnerships. Fear is partially responsible for not planning or discovering vision. On the other hand, a different attitude about fear can become a positive.

The Strong and The Weak, by Paul Tournier, writes:

> *"No endeavor is fruitful without fear ...Fear is Universal because it is an instinct...It is fear of everything new which gives personal and social life its stability and the framework of habits without which all is confusion."*

Tournier reminds us of the grasp that fear has on life, but when fear is seen as "stability" then there is hope. Discovering vision leads to controlling the fear in a way that it becomes "stability". People with fears describe the feeling sometimes as having butterflies in the stomach. Since fear is instinct, controlling fear is taking the butterflies and putting them into formation. What is the motivation for controlling fear? The motivation for controlling fear is in the words, "Love never ends." If the marital base is rooted in this belief, then couples will find a vision for the future.

ASPIRING A VISION

> *"Faith is love taking the form of aspiration."*
>
> WILLIAM ELLERY CHANNING

"Tis immortality to die aspiring."

GEORGE CHAPMAN

"Aspirations after the holy—the only aspirations in which the soul can be assured it will never meet with disappointment."

MARIA MCINTOSH

Where might aspiration begin? Maybe appreciation? A couple decided to sell their home, so they brought in a realtor to make an assessment of the value of the property. The realtor listed the property, and wrote an ad for the newspaper describing the home and area of location. The ad included an excellent description relating to the good points, and describing the beauty of the landscaping, plus the house. After reading the ad, the couple looked at each other, and exclaimed, "We don't want to sell. This is a great place to live!"

How much does it take to appreciate the material world a couple might already have in possessions? Too often there is a blindness in seeking, in other words, aspiring for more "things." Looking at the "things" already possessed, might remind partners to vision beyond the material world. In a world where the few have so much, and the many have so little, certainly the vision must be higher than the ground people live and walk on.

Aspiring "after the holy" might just be the ticket to that immortality humans hope for after life has absorbed the physical to its very limits intended by the Creator. The spiritual takes precedence over the material when life comes down to its finality. Physical dies, but spiritual lives. It's immortal.

Places of worship provide multiple opportunities for partners to pursue the route of spiritual journeys. Although institutional religion has lost its savor for some, nevertheless, in spite of imperfections, it is still a good place to begin. Congregations do provide ways of spiritual support, and in the dire needs of life's unexpected turns, helps provide a source of faith development as well as faith support. An appreciation of religious values contributes to the kind of love that endures and promotes vision.

A couple in counseling was asked about their "secret" for maintaining a long and rather happy marriage. Both came to the same conclusion: "Faith helped plan our future, and our future became a part of our present, and our present proves the need to aspire beyond the material things of life, and the result is happiness."

Several years ago a pre-marital clinic for engaged couples required they mark on a separate printed sheet their attitudes toward basics including the following: religion, family, work, and children. Then they compared their results. Of course most of the answers did not match, so the next step asked the couples to communicate how they would adjust to the differences. This is a good exercise because the adjustments reveal the true aspirations of reaching goals for the future. Goal or visions, depending on your concept, also need continued adjustments along the way. Taking time to make a change indicates the aspiring couple is determined to make the most and the best of the relationship.

Relationships are not expected to reach agreements on everything, especially vision for the future. Individuals change, and develop differently within a partnership. As previously mentioned, children bring a whole new dimension to marriage. People are blessed when children arrive, but at times the newborn child is not always healthy. This demands a totally new approach to the future. Such an example is only one way in which life changes directions for us, whether couples want to or not. The example may be extreme, however, the strength needed to cope with unexpected challenges of life needs aspiration way beyond the material. Some challenges of life can never be prepared for, even with the best minds. Common sense knows well the results.

> *"We read the past by the light of the present, and the forms vary as the shadows fall, or as the point of the vision alters."*
>
> JAMES ANTHONY FROUDE, WRITER

LIVING THE VISION

> *"A vision without a task is a dream;*
> *A task without a vision is drudgery;*
> *A vision and a task is the hope of the world."*
>
> ANONYMOUS

Living the vision seeks to achieve, through efforts, the reality of dreaming and planning. Successful relationships are further bonded by the efforts. Reality is the success of the vision. Marriages that rely on chance will not likely have happy results. Gambling on happiness should not become the favorite pastime.

Jesus said, "...search, and you will find; knock, and the door will be opened for you." Matthew 7:7 (NRSV). Searching and knocking are keys to the reality of the vision. Successful people do not wait until "something" happens before taking action. Partnerships that want action rather than reaction, find ways to live out the dream.

James Allen wrote, "The strength of the effort is the measure of the result." Results are the "proof in the pudding", so to say. They also provide the yardstick for measuring the strength, that is, time and energy, placed on living the vision. Visions tend to get lost along the way, especially when time and energy are absorbed by daily responsibilities. A "planning day" might appear to be too structured for some, but the idea of taking special moments, at minimum, will assist in keeping focus on the dreams.

Gloom and doom come to some of the best partnerships when losing a focus on the dreams is lost. Some blame failures in losing dreams on the circumstances of life. Certainly the setbacks are natural, but the love that is real is a love that endures and maintains the dreams. Losing the dreams loses the realities.

"The greatest achievement was at first and for a time a dream.
The oak sleeps in the acorn; the bird waits in the egg; and in
The highest vision of the soul a waking angel stirs.
Dreams are the seedlings of realities."

JAMES ALLEN, WRITER

SUMMARY

Married couples need to broaden their vision of life together. Discovering a vision in marital life involves the ability to see beyond today. Life evolves and needs to be comprehended in the "becoming."

A fear of the future is a large obstacle in the success of partnerships. Planning ahead will not only broaden marital adventures, but will also brighten them as well. The couple that really believes "love never ends" will find a vision in their future.

Aspiring to a vision is motivated by "love never ends." Aspiring to a vision means looking toward the spiritual as well as the material. Material goals alone tend to destroy the best of relationships. Appreciating what couples already possess leads to more emphasis on the spiritual.

In order for dreams to become realities then efforts are needed. Waiting for the future to take its own course could end in a lack of the true happiness partnerships are seeking. Searching and knocking are the keys to helping dreams become realities.

The beauty of married life comes in the discovering the vision, aspiring to the vision, and living the vision. Such beauty assures that "love never ends."

DISCUSSION QUESTIONS

FUTURE

Discovering The Vision

1. Why is it necessary for partners to have a vision?
2. What are some ways to discover a vision?
3. Discuss some major obstacles to discovering vision together?
4. What motivations would one perceive in planning for the future?
5. How does "Love never ends" become a motivator for the future?

Aspiring To The Vision

1. What possessions do you not appreciate?
2. How is appreciation effective in aspiring to a vision?
3. What is the value in aspiring to spiritual things?
4. How does the spiritual value relate to a successful relationship?
5. What effect can unexpected changes have on a vision?

Living The Vision

1. What is the purpose of searching and knocking?
2. Discuss the importance of applying efforts to living a vision.
3. Discuss James Allen's "Dreams are the seedlings of realities."
4. What might be the penalty of leaving a vision in a marriage to chance?
5. How might a couple regain a lost vision?

11

OLD-FASIONED RECIPES FOR KEEPING THE KNOT TIED

DAILY PREPARATION:

Use more than a "pinch" of kindness with a cup of caring.
Use more than a "gulup" of respect with a cup of sharing.
Use more than a "tad" of truth with a cup of forgiving.
Use more than a "dash" of endurance with a cup of giving.
Use more than a "sprinkle" of vision with a cup of believing.

JOHN H. GREEN, PH.D.

WISDOM:

Two checkbooks
Two bathrooms
One bed

ANONYMOUS

HAPPINESS:

One tablespoon of loving
One whole longing for desire
One teaspoon of satisfaction
One cup of compassionate florets
One-third cup of "May I, please?"
One-quarter tablespoon of "Certainly, I love you!"
One date per week, minimum
One celebration per quarter, minimum
Two ribs meeting day or night, heavenly!

JOHN H. GREEN, PH.D.

BIBLICAL RECIPES

"He that is married cares for the things that are of the world, how he may please his wife." She that is married cares for the things of the world, how she may please her husband." I Corinthians 7:33-34

"These things I command you, that you love one another." John 15:17

"Love eliminates a multitude of sins." I Peter 4:8

"If you love not, then you do not love God." I John 4:8

INSPIRATIONAL RECIPES

"Love is not blind. Lust is blind. If love is blind, God is blind."

GORDON PALMER, WRITER

"Force may subdue, but love gains, and he who forgives first wins the laurel."

WILLIAM PENN

"To love as Christ loves is to let our love be a practical and not a sentimental love."

SIR CHARLES STANFORD

"There is a land of the living, and land of the dead, and the bridge is love."

THORNTON WILDE

"Transferring the love from my heart to your heart can be done without surgery. Thanks to Jesus, the Great Physician."

JOHN H. GREEN, PH.D.

12

MESSAGES OF LOVE AFTER TYING THE KNOT

LOVE IS PATIENT

Substitute God for "Love", and you get "God is patient." God is so patient that He never gives up on his creation. Books of the Old Testament like Jonah, Isaiah, Jeremiah, and others, just to name a few, remind readers that God seeks His people. God runs after us relentlessly until His creation stops, turns, and embraces the love of the Creator. God continues to run after us with astounding patience. Some feel they have found God at times in their lives, when in fact, God finds them through His undying reluctance to give up on His creation.

God's patience is evident in the New Testament as one quickly recognizes Jesus is in the face of God. Jesus is patient. The parable of the Lost Sheep and the parable of the Prodigal Son, among many, remind us of the patient and seeking God. In the Parable of the Lost Sheep, the Shepherd is not satisfied to have ninety-nine out of a hundred sheep. The Shepherd goes searching for the one lost until found. Patience reigns as a characteristic of the Shepherd. The Parable of the Prodigal Son reflects on the joy of the Father waiting for the sinful son to come home, and greets the son by embracing him with love and forgiveness. The joy of finding one lost, and the return of one lost in his ways, represent the greatest evidence of a caring, loving, and seeking Creator. Obviously God is a very patient Creator.

The Holy Spirit is patient. God's presence is identified as a Holy Spirit. The Holy Spirit represents God's everlasting patience. The Holy Spirit is so patient that creatures are allowed the spirit of free will, the flexibility to make mistakes and errors of life with the opportunity of forgiveness. The motive of the free will decisions can only be determined and judged by the Holy Spirit, and therefore rationalization can't be confused with the truth of one's repentance. There is an old saying, "A mistake is not an error unless you fail to correct it." The Holy Spirit, representing the presence of God, allows for the mistake to be corrected, or in some instances, re-routed to replace sin with good. The everlasting grace of

God, amazing grace of God, teaches the everlasting patience, amazing patience of God, to those who would believe and allow the better decisions and choices of life granted by free will.

The flexibility to change is an important ingredient in the mix of life. Life displays us in ways that choices for a lifetime are more and more important. The choice to apply for the right job will come along. A choice of gaining knowledge through education is always available to those with the best decisions. The choice of a person to marry requires patience. True love is patient.

LOVE IS KIND

God is kind. Kindness is the undeniable proof of Christian love. Patience unveils its presence in the face of kindness. One of the root meanings of the Greek word for kindness is respect. Respect too often reveals the lost concept of being kind. Kindness loses its reign over all creatures when a cup of water is refused to the thirsty, or food is refused to the hungry, or clothing is refused to a naked one, or a visit is refused to a prison inmate.

Acts of kindness done "in the name of Jesus" is the same as witnessing to His Spirit. Kindness moves beyond the self and into a realm of selflessness. A friendly smile, a word of cheer, the mildly clinching handshake; all truly symbolize the very nature of a living God. The fire of the Holy Spirit is kindled in the acts of kindness.

Kindness has a way of leveling the playing field of life. As the world spins out of control with religious conflicts spreading across the world, and with God's creatures bent on destroying one another, the acts of kindness have a tendency to bring all into perspective, and demonstrate the need to look beyond the hubris expressions of hate, and believe that a better world is for the having when people of all faiths begin living the words, "Love is kind."

Love creates an atmosphere of fairness as well as kindness. Looking beyond the petty, selfish will, in which God's creatures might treat one another, is the heavenly vision of revealing that everybody's shadow is the same color! Nowhere in the world does the sun make a person's shadow a different color. All of God's creatures are the same no matter the culture, religion, or governmental structure found across the known world when shadows are compared! In faith people are created in the image of the Creator who made heaven and earth, including the sun. The sun reveals that shadows are equal, no matter where one travels across the known terrain. This equality commands that respect, love, and the birth of kindness be as equal to all as to one.

The credit card company reminds customers of the material costs of "things", but there is a more significant part to life that is priceless. Treating others in a manner of hatred, and not love, is the highest cost of disharmony in the world, indicating a love for "things", while treating others with love, not hate, creates that which is priceless. When "Love is kind" then life is priceless.

Moving beyond the world of disharmony takes a strong fortitude that develops into a strong courage of standing one's ground when it comes to believing in kindness. Why? Because kindness is the enemy of the of all that stands for evil in the world. Being kind takes away the defenses of evil, and provides a resurrection of the good life.

LOVE IS NOT RUDE

The display of good manners is more than a small virtue. Virtues may come in sizes for some, but in certain situations, small seems big. It is worthy to note that Jesus set the standard for good manners. How thoughtfully Jesus responded when the women touched the hem of his garment! How forcefully he responded in the defense he gave to the woman when she was about to be stoned for adultery! His sensitivity and understanding displayed the highest standard of good manners. And, again, how sensitive Jesus was when he defended the woman who was derided by the disciples when she poured expensive oil over Jesus! She even washed his feet with her tears.

To those who were so ready to criticize, in essence, Jesus said, "Mind your manners!" Jesus' attitude was not jealous, boastful, arrogant, or rude. Humility guides lovers to be aware of virtuous manners. True love sets the standards for humble beginnings. No love is so weak and fragile that it cannot muster up the essence of good manners.

Those who would display poor manners today do so in many other ways as well. Cell phone use, poor driving habits, and the simple measure of complaining because the line is too long, might qualify for the practice of simply good manners.

Cell phone users have evolved into the most obnoxious people around by talking, sometimes very loudly, almost anywhere at any time, without regards to other people's rights. Inside the restaurant, while driving, and in the public bathrooms! How insensitive can one be who has no sensitivity to others? Mind your manners!

Poor driving habits are not always the result of using the cell phone. Putting on makeup, smoking, reading a map or the newspaper, contribute to many an automobile accidents. Road rage, for cutting someone off at the pass, so to speak, contributes to disaster, too often, death. Good manners are no small virtues.

Standing in line is not fun, but good manners have been displayed by unkind words, shoving, and down right meanness. People have fought over "breaking in line" for theaters, sports events, restaurants, and numerous other occasions. Rudeness, arrogance, and jealousy too often contribute to the downfall of good character and, in turn, good manners.

So, one can easily qualify good manners as more than just a small virtue. The small may become large when the person allows emotions to override sensibility. The lack of sensibility and sensitivity may lead to outcomes that trigger unlimited avenues of rudeness, arrogance, boastfulness, and jealousy. Minding one's manners can be a positive contrast to the need to hurt and defy the rights of others. Freedoms must include the respect of the rights of others. Mind your manners!

LOVE DOES NOT INSIST ON ITS OWN WAY

Self-assertiveness is not the same as self-serving or selfishness. The first is positive and, sometimes, becomes the only way to stand up for one's rights. The latter, on the other hand, is extremely negative and, most often, contributes to hurt feelings, and permanent damage to relationships. Insisting on one's own way leads to the possible inability to head off the kind of resentfulness that causes total breakdown between people, leaving out the opportunity of healing the damage. Self-assertiveness is nowhere near the same as self-serving or selfishness.

Self-assertiveness actually protects one from the selfish people. A defense is needed, sometimes required, in order to stand up to the crowd or individual who would otherwise run over a person due to self-serving intentions. Self-assertiveness wards off those who would be resentful and irritable due to their own selfish needs. At work, home, or school, the desire to control your life by others is best combated by self-assertiveness. There is a big difference between standing up for oneself and living only for oneself. The difference makes the difference in one's character, and thereby one's destiny in life.

Sometimes the self-serving creature has to look into the mirror to see they are being selfish. Relationships cover up the truth if one member of the relationship creates a falsehood by being unassertive. Thinking that not challenging another's selfish behavior will keep harmony in a relationship can lead to a masking of the truth. Sometimes the neglect of not showing the troublemaker the mirror of self, simply delays the inevitable, and leads to a more permanent disharmony, or even worse, a totally dysfunctional relationship.

True love works at becoming unselfish. Work is a key word. The need to take care of self reigns supreme when there is an attitude that it will simply happen. Taking care of self needs directions – selfishness or self-assertive? Most likely, one or the other doesn't just happen. Unhealthy fighting occurs when the irritable and the resentful take over. When a relationship does not "work" at the core of the problem of selfishness, then the irritable and resentful take charge, and the avenues to love and peace are closed for a long time, or forever.

Jesus is the antithesis to self-serving. Following the life of Jesus reveals a path of self-assertiveness and not selfishness. His teaching to the disciples is evident in his call to serve others and not self. He was assertive when charged that he had violated the Sabbath in Jewish law by saying, "The Sabbath is not made for man, but man was made for the Sabbath." This came about when the disciples were hungry and it was the Sabbath, but they gathered corn to eat. Jesus stood up for that right. Being hungry is not selfish, and taking the lead to see that others have food is assertiveness.

LOVE DOES NOT REJOICE IN WRONGDOING

There is a desire to divide all of human actions into right or wrong or black or white. Shades of gray seem less correct and not acceptable to perfect people.

However, motives appear to be left out of the perfect equation. Therefore, all things considered, the motives of an individual are to be judged by the Creator. Actions might appear to be the basis for judgment, but the actions don't tell all. Some might say that is rationalization and not getting at the truth. The Creator knows the difference between rationalization and the truth, making the Creator's judgment the most important.

"No one is perfect and all fall short of the glory of God," according to the Apostle Paul. This readily relates to the teaching of Jesus. Jesus knew everyone had faults, but he was attracted to the best qualities in each individual. Those best qualities seemed to him to be the focus point of the imperfect life.

Jesus chose fishermen to follow him in spreading the word, not the Priests. He marveled at the faith of a Roman Centurian who placed his faith in God. Jesus asked the disciples to emulate the faith of the widow who gave all she had at the Temple, known as the Widow's Mite. He saw the "queen" in the harlot. Where many saw water, Jesus saw wine. He was the Author of discovery in finding the good in people.

Every human creation hungers to be treated as if there is potential in their lives for good. Children prosper when they are taught the truth, and not to rejoice in wrongdoing, but they prosper even more knowing there is forgiveness for wrongdoing. Mother Teresa saw a special gift in every living person, and sought to provide for that individual, good or bad, or a little of both, a way to let Jesus enter their lives. No matter the sin she had the gift of serving the ordinary folks, and making them as worthy as the "angels" in heaven. Even in the midst of their suffering she walked and talked the grace of Jesus.

Treating each other in a relationship with dignity and integrity will allow the truth to thrive. Wrongdoing will find a door to leave when the honor of a person is restored. Humans naturally long for the spiritual dimension that will direct their lives in a manner that upholds the highest of standards, often after a wrong has been committed. If wrong rules right, then make it temporary. Get back up on the horse and ride, so to speak, so that right will eventually rule over wrong.

Infidelity is wrongdoing, and no amount of rationalization will make the immoral act right. Relationships might need to end rather than the continued practice of infidelity. At least one partner will be able to start over with someone who has a higher level of truth. Two wrongs will not make a right. Staying in an unhealthy relationship plagued by infidelity, just to keep the partnership, asks for a life of misery. Restore truth. Move on!

LOVE BEARS ALL THINGS

There is a thought that love actually covers all things. The "covers" protect from the chill of the winter's cold. Covers, like a tent, protect from the mist or rainfall at a social time or while camping. Covers, as metaphor, protect us from the challenges of life. The ills and chills of life, such as the uncontrolled disasters of life and the tribulations of life, are challenged by the Jesus of the

Cross. Love creates support, and support fosters courage, and courage gives the strength to meet the challenges. And, all challenges, from the emotional, to the psychological, to the financial, are all covered by the love that "bears all things."

Jesus knows, through the cross, our grief and feels our sorrows because Jesus bears all things. Jesus was born and lived in a world of tension, confusion, and troubled times. Today has its own troubles to bear, and is hardly different because the world still needs strength and courage to meet the challenges. The world needs the "covers" to protect from the cold wind chill factors of living. Thousands die everyday in our world needing and crying for a cover of love that will support them. Challenges can be conquered by the power of the cross.

Support is a key word in the needs of human beings. Left alone without the support of friends or family is a devastating trial of life. The lonely are often the elderly who, unfortunately, are left to be cared for by others outside the family. Needless to say, there are situations where the needs cannot be met at home, and that could be detrimental to the patient. Therefore, a situation dictates the need for the help beyond the home. However, numerous studies indicate that too many times the patient is seldom, if ever, visited on a regular basis when placed in a nursing home. Loneliness, from a lack of emotional and spiritual support, creates depression to the point another pill has to be given to combat the emotional instability. Leaving a dear love one uncovered reveals a horrific attitude toward the elderly that is, more than borderline, disgraceful.

Christian responsibility commands attention to the care and love of one another regardless of age. Included in the need for protective covers are our children. Child abuse, physical and sexual, represents one of the most disturbing problems in today's world. And it is the world, not just in one country. Some countries continue to harbor children as victims of slave trade, child labor, and sexual objects. The cry from Jesus is to bring to justice the terrible crimes against children in this seedy and decadent society. If one does believe in a Day of Judgment, then surely one realizes the crimes against children will be eventually brought to justice, but that is no excuse not to something now. The Jesus of the Cross cries aloud to help these poor, innocent victims, and the words of Jesus could not be more relevant than today, "Suffer the little children unto me for such is the Kingdom of God."

LOVE HOPES ALL THINGS

The parable of the Prodigal Son reminds one that the wayward son was still loved by the father. The erring woman that Jesus met at the well, for water, confessed to the truth that she had five husbands, and was still given hope by Jesus. He accepted a cool drink of water from her, and then promised her the water of life that she might never be thirsty again. Hope comes when the down and out are brought up and into the fold of love. Hope is never lost in the presence of Jesus. Jesus opens the eyes of those who have lost all hope. He makes one "stretch" beyond the normal capacity to reach what might seem to be at the time, the impossible.

What Jesus did for others was not magic or manipulative, but simply put, magnificent! Hope brings magnificent happenings beyond, well often, belief. Hope inspires the helpless to look at life in a different perspective, and to change the attitude in order to lead life in a different direction. It is finding the new direction that provides the ability of a human being to look beyond oneself.

True friendship often assists in leading one on the paths of hope. A lost person can be found when a dear friend cares enough to provide assistance for a new direction. Jesus is also a friend, as he said to his disciples, "You are my friends." One of the favorite hymns of the faith records, "What a Friend we have in Jesus, all our sins and grief to bear, what a privilege to carry everything to him in prayer." When there is an emphatic listening person who responds with love and care, there is hope.

The parable of the Lost Sheep, reveals that "one" lost is just as important as the "ninety-nine" sheep present. The Shepherd seeks the "one" with all the passion and desire to save as if there were ninety-nine lost. Jesus is the Shepherd and those who profess Jesus become shepherds to those who are lost. Lost is a word used for a lost soul most often, but should be applied to those lost in a world that is moving so fast it is hard to keep up. Lack of medical attention, dysfunctional families, and on-going wars, to name a few, have placed people on a lost island needing the help of a Good Shepherd.

The special creatures of heaven and earth, created in the image of God, but lost in the creation, are actively sought by the Good Shepherd. God's image, reflected in Jesus, seeks to find and transform the lives of creatures in order that hope becomes the major factor in life, and not hopelessness. Even if you don't seek God, God is seeking each and every person. One can run, but one cannot hide from the power of the One who creates and KEEPS the creation. Looking beyond life on earth is the One who offers an eternal hope beyond the comprehension of some, but not beyond the realm of the Creator. Therein lies the Creator's eternal hope!

LOVE BELIEVES ALL THINGS

Attitude often rules the roost, so to speak, in helping make life's burdens easier to control. A very poor attitude diminishes the quality of life, and eliminates the fun needed in living a healthy life. Believing provides a level of love and trust that presents timely relief in pronouncing an enjoyable life. Jesus said, "I have come that you might have life and have it more abundantly." Choice words for a Prophet who taught that life is for living the best moments that may never come again on earth. Jesus was not without time of relaxation and meditation. Fun? Well, yes. An attitude is built through a mindset and feelings of worthiness and security. His examples of finding time with "his friends" to fish, eat, attend weddings, and seek moments of solitude away from the crowds, provided for him and his friends many moments of appreciating life through relaxation and meditation, and thus, a worthy attitude.

Love has a way of encouraging people to stop, and as heard many times, "smell the roses;" and do it more often than less. Literature, music, all forms of art, and different styles of worship provide many outlets for relieving the pinned up tensions and other emotions of the day, and employ an attitude that makes for more positive outlook on daily routines. Believing assists in providing a sense of harmony within the realities of living. Very seldom does one have the strength to tarry on without some form of entertainment. Americans, in particular, take the fewest vacations. Some British acquaintances could not believe the few days of vacation that Americans normally take in a year's time. Certainly some worship the "work ethic" as though it was a god of sorts. There is high regard for work ethics in America, and should not be taken lightly, but "all work and no play does make Jack a dull boy!"

Jesus always saw the potential in people. He encouraged them with God's grace, and the love of a formidable parent, to teach the necessities of life, including a sense of believing beyond oneself. That sense may be stored within us looking for a way of expression, and when there is no outlet for expressing these inherent feelings, then negative emotional explosions take place. Anger, fear, and simply put, meanness, erupts like a volcanic action to dominate our lives, and thereby, destroy our natural potential to be what Jesus saw in human beings.

What Jesus saw was an undying possibility that people can accomplish their needs of life, when believing in him. The potential he saw overrode the mistakes made. His philosophy of grace might be this simple: "An error is not a mistake until you fail to correct it." Living life without relaxation and meditation will take its toll on the individual to the point where too many errors are made, and there is no longer time or energy to correct them. Jesus brought love to the level that releases one from sin, anxieties, daily problems, and offers the opportunities and possibilities for abundant living in the place of these unfortunate times of life.

LOVE ENDURES ALL THINGS

When the ground becomes quicksand for one's faith, and there is no ground firm enough for hope, love, the greatest of these, will manage to endure. Endurance will pull faith out of the quicksand. There is permanence in the action of love. Even though there are moments when one's back is to the wall, there follows a steadfastness that creates the endurance to survive with the knowledge of love. Jesus is love.

Jesus said, "But he who endures to the end will be saved." (Matthew 10:22 – NRSV) This is the permanence that provides stability to the faint hearted. Jesus takes the burdens of life, and brings a person to the point where one can rejoice with the hymn, "Love Lifted Me." When NOTHING else can help, love is the endurance prescribed. Comfort for the weary is a major outcome when love endures. Jesus is love.

Emotional pains sometimes emerge from the happenings of the day. Often the pain is neglected too long before the need for help is realized. But when a person moves quickly to deal with emotional pain, the results can be more satisfying.

Satisfaction is recognizing the trust level is stronger, and that love has a way of stabilizing the happenings.

Controlling the emotional pains is not the same as concealing the pains. Concealing the pains leads to emotional breakdowns. Controlling the pains is dealing with the problems, maybe with professional counseling, but always with a faith, hope, and love. Professional counseling is often needed to aid in keeping a healthy endurance level. It may be the supplement that provides the openness to accept faith, hope, and love. Counseling is not a negative, but a positive approach when the burdens are too heavy.

Marriages, partnerships, or on-going friendships, might encounter extraordinary amounts of hurt and emotional pain, due to the closeness of the relationship. The unexpected sufferings, like automobile accidents and deaths, might also bring on the most unwelcome pains. However, when there is a strong bond between people, coupled with faith, hope, and love, there will form a security and, in spite of the unexpected challenges of life, this bond will endure. If there is no foundation of faith, hope, or love, then the consequences of the tragic moments will be unbearable. Jesus is the Cornerstone in the foundation, and assures all who would come unto him will be loved. The Jesus for all seasons is the Jesus of love.

LOVE NEVER ENDS

Love is evanescent. Sound impressive? Well, that is to say love is very impressive when people share the knowledge that love is never ending. "Having loved his own who were in the world, he loved them to the end." (John 13:1- NRSV) This characteristic is vividly illustrated in the relationship between Jesus and his followers. No one who believed in him was able to go beyond his boundaries of love. Grace is the forgiveness of sins, and love is grace.

Sometimes grace is under pressure because forgiving is not always easy. Forgiving does not mean forgetting. Some relationships are destroyed with breaking the bonds of trust. Breaking the bonds of trust may lead to the point of no return. Forgetting is more often deemed impossible at the point of no return, but forgiveness should never be deemed impossible. Jesus is forgiveness. In the act of forgiveness love never ends.

Even in death nothing separates Jesus from his beloved people. Jesus is stronger than death. He transcended death through the power of love as experienced in the story of the resurrection of Jesus. The resurrection opened the door to the identity of Jesus as one who loved and died that God's evolving purpose of life might be revealed. The resurrection of Jesus is the revelation of God's perfect nature.

The assurance of the One who knows suffering, and the One who gives eternal life, provides all who believe the power to live without fear. Fear freezes the heart and the soul and can only be conquered by the power of unending love. An unending love never falters or wanes. Even death cannot change anything when the power of love produces eternity. Jesus is life.

www.ingramcontent.com/pod-product-compliance
Ingram Content Group UK Ltd.
Pitfield, Milton Keynes, MK11 3LW, UK
UKHW020139250726
13967UKWH00002B/758

9 781425 182779